W9-AZR-265

DK CHILDREN'S
ILLUSTRATED REFERENCE
ATLAS

Brian Delf

LONDON, NEW YORK, MUNICH,
MELBOURNE, DELHI

Editor Lorrie Mack
Designers Adrienne Hutchinson, Andrew O'Brien
Jacket Design David McDonald
DTP Designer Jill Bunyan, David McDonald
Design Manager Jane Thomas
Managing Editor Andrew Macintyre
Production Sarah Hughes

The material in this book originally appeared in the
Picture Atlas of the World, published in 1991

With thanks to the original team:
Lester Cheeseman, Marcus James, Emma Johnson,
Richard Kemp, Keith Lye, Susan Peach, Roger Priddy,
Teresa Solomon, Kate Woodward, Anna Kunst,
Chris Scollen, Richard Czapnik, Struan Reid,
Cynthia Hole and Luciano Corbella

Published in Great Britain in 2008
by Dorling Kindersley Limited,
80 Strand, London WC2R 0RL
A Penguin company

This edition copyright © 2002, 2008
Dorling Kindersley, Limited
Picture Atlas of the World copyright © 1991, 1992
Dorling Kindersley, Limited

All rights reserved. No part of this publication may
be reproduced, stored in a retrieval system, or transmitted
in any form or by any means, electronic, mechanical,
photocopying, recording, or otherwise, without prior
written permission of the copyright owner.

A CIP catalogue record for this book is available
from the British Library.

ISBN   978-1-4053-4290-2

Colour reproduction by Bright Arts, Hong Kong
Printed and bound in China by Toppan

Picture credits
(r = right, l = left, t = top, c = centre, b = bottom)

Australian Overseas Information Service, London 45tr, 45br;
Charles Bowman 22t, 22b, 35tr, 35br, 46t; Caribbean Tourist Office
27t; The J. Allan Cash Photolibrary 8tl, 8br, 17tl, 46br;
Lester Cheeseman 37tl, 37tr, 37bc; Chinese Tourist Office 23br;
Egyptian Tourist Office 33tr; Chris Fairclough Colour Library 15tr,
15br, 17r; French Railways Ltd 11cr; Italian State Tourist Office 20t;
Norwegian Tourist Office 6tr, 7tr; Roger Priddy 8tr, 11tr, 11br, 46t;
Spanish National Tourist Office 19tr; The Telegraph Colour Library
13b; Travel Photo International 15br, 19b.

Every effort has been made to trace the copyright holders
and we apologise in advance for any unintentional omissions.
We would be pleased to insert the appropriate acknowledgment
in any subsequent edition of this book.

Discover more at
www.dk.com

CONTENTS

KEY TO THE MAPS

Capital city	**BERLIN** ★
City	● **Toronto**
Country name	**JAPAN**
Range of mountains	*ALPS*
An individual mountain with its height	MT EVEREST 8,850 M
River	*Danube*
Lake	LAKE COMO
A building or place of special interest	LEANING TOWER OF PISA
A product, animal, plant or activity that is found in the region	*Dairy cattle*

WORLD MAP

ALL THE CONTINENTS except Antarctica are divided into countries, and these vary greatly in size. The largest is the Russian Federation, which stretches across two continents – Europe and Asia. The second largest is Canada, and the third largest is China. In contrast, the smallest country is Vatican City, which lies inside the city of Rome and has an area of only 0.44 sq km (0.17 sq miles). The Russian Federation is almost 39 million times bigger than Vatican City.

LATITUDE AND LONGITUDE
Geographers draw imaginary lines around the globe to help locate places. Lines of latitude run east/west and are measured in degrees from the Equator. Lines of longitude run north/south and are measured in degrees from the Prime Meridian.

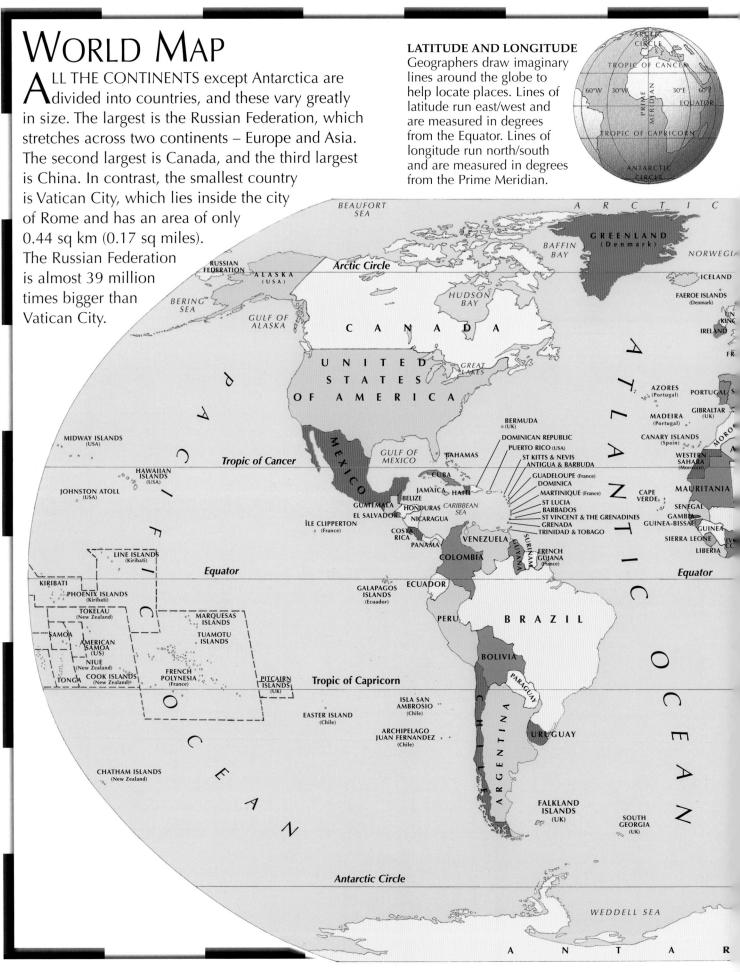

BEAUFORT SEA
ARCTIC
GREENLAND (Denmark)
BAFFIN BAY
NORWEGIA
RUSSIAN FEDERATION
Arctic Circle
ALASKA (USA)
ICELAND
BERING SEA
HUDSON BAY
FAEROE ISLANDS (Denmark)
GULF OF ALASKA
C A N A D A
UN
KING
IRELAND
U N I T E D
S T A T E S
GREAT LAKES
O F   A M E R I C A
ATLANTIC
FR
AZORES (Portugal)
PORTUGAL S.
BERMUDA (UK)
GIBRALTAR (UK)
MADEIRA (Portugal)
MORO
MIDWAY ISLANDS (USA)
DOMINICAN REPUBLIC
PUERTO RICO (USA)
CANARY ISLANDS (Spain)
Tropic of Cancer
GULF OF MEXICO
BAHAMAS
ST KITTS & NEVIS
ANTIGUA & BARBUDA
WESTERN SAHARA (Morocco)
HAWAIIAN ISLANDS (USA)
CUBA
GUADELOUPE (France)
MAURITANIA
JOHNSTON ATOLL (USA)
MEXICO
JAMAICA
HAITI
DOMINICA
MARTINIQUE (France)
CAPE VERDE
SENEGAL
GUATEMALA
BELIZE
HONDURAS
CARIBBEAN SEA
ST LUCIA
BARBADOS
GAMBIA
GUINEA-BISSAU
GUINEA
ÎLE CLIPPERTON (France)
EL SALVADOR
NICARAGUA
ST VINCENT & THE GRENADINES
GRENADA
TRINIDAD & TOBAGO
SIERRA LEONE
IV
CC
COSTA RICA
PANAMA
VENEZUELA
SURINAM
FRENCH GUIANA (France)
LIBERIA
LINE ISLANDS (Kiribati)
COLOMBIA
Equator
Equator
GALAPAGOS ISLANDS (Ecuador)
ECUADOR
KIRIBATI
PHOENIX ISLANDS (Kiribati)
PERU
B R A Z I L
TOKELAU (New Zealand)
MARQUESAS ISLANDS
SAMOA
TUAMOTU ISLANDS
AMERICAN SAMOA (US)
BOLIVIA
NIUE (New Zealand)
FRENCH POLYNESIA (France)
PITCAIRN ISLANDS (UK)
Tropic of Capricorn
PARAGUAY
TONGA
COOK ISLANDS (New Zealand)
ISLA SAN AMBROSIO (Chile)
URUGUAY
EASTER ISLAND (Chile)
ARCHIPELAGO JUAN FERNANDEZ (Chile)
CHILE
ARGENTINA
CHATHAM ISLANDS (New Zealand)
O C E A N
FALKLAND ISLANDS (UK)
SOUTH GEORGIA (UK)
P A C I F I C
Antarctic Circle
WEDDELL SEA
A N T A R

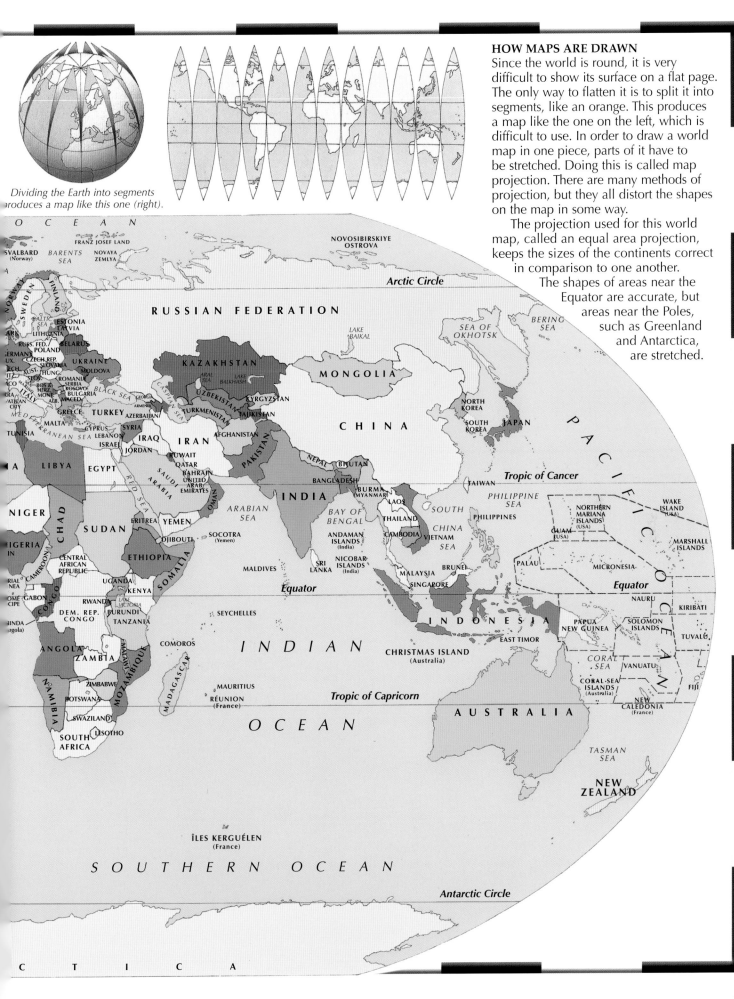

Dividing the Earth into segments produces a map like this one (right).

HOW MAPS ARE DRAWN

Since the world is round, it is very difficult to show its surface on a flat page. The only way to flatten it is to split it into segments, like an orange. This produces a map like the one on the left, which is difficult to use. In order to draw a world map in one piece, parts of it have to be stretched. Doing this is called map projection. There are many methods of projection, but they all distort the shapes on the map in some way.

The projection used for this world map, called an equal area projection, keeps the sizes of the continents correct in comparison to one another.

The shapes of areas near the Equator are accurate, but areas near the Poles, such as Greenland and Antarctica, are stretched.

THE ARCTIC

The arctic circle contains parts of North America, Europe and Asia, and most of Greenland. Within it, there are winter days when the sun never rises, and summer days when it never sets. Much of the ocean is permanently frozen, but despite the climate, many animals and plants live in the Arctic. The main human inhabitants are the Inuit (Eskimos) and the Sami (Lapps).

Greenland is anything but green – it is largely covered by ice. The Inuit settled there in about 2500 BC; the first Europeans, the Vikings, arrived in about AD 986. Today, Greenland is a province of Denmark.

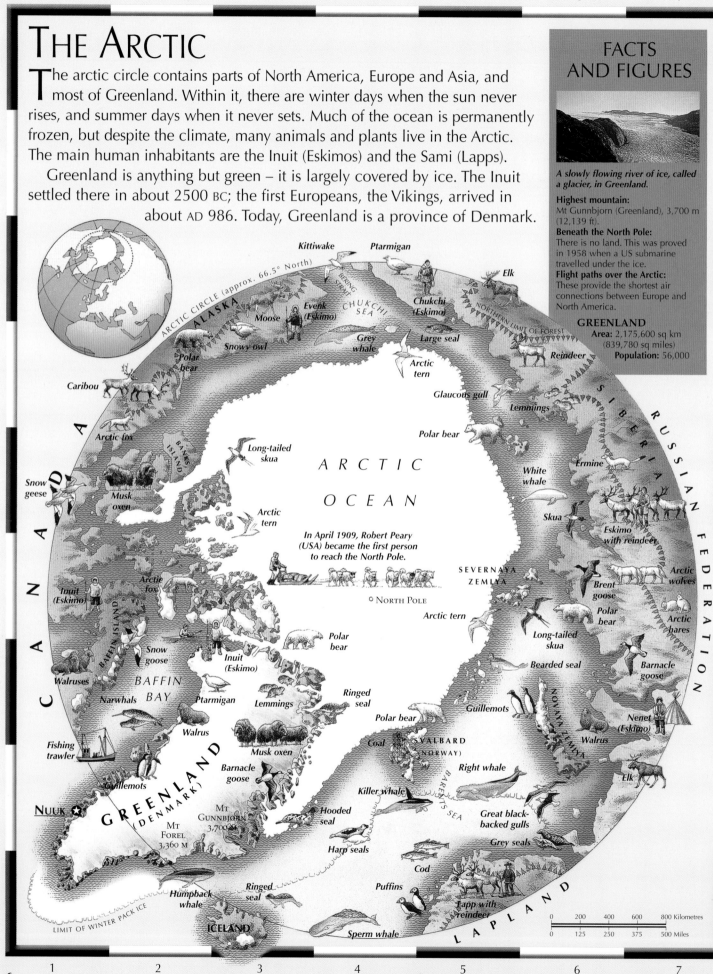

FACTS AND FIGURES

A slowly flowing river of ice, called a glacier, in Greenland.

Highest mountain:
Mt Gunnbjorn (Greenland), 3,700 m (12,139 ft)
Beneath the North Pole:
There is no land. This was proved in 1958 when a US submarine travelled under the ice.
Flight paths over the Arctic:
These provide the shortest air connections between Europe and North America.

GREENLAND
Area: 2,175,600 sq km (839,780 sq miles)
Population: 56,000

In April 1909, Robert Peary (USA) became the first person to reach the North Pole.

ARCTIC OCEAN

NORTH POLE

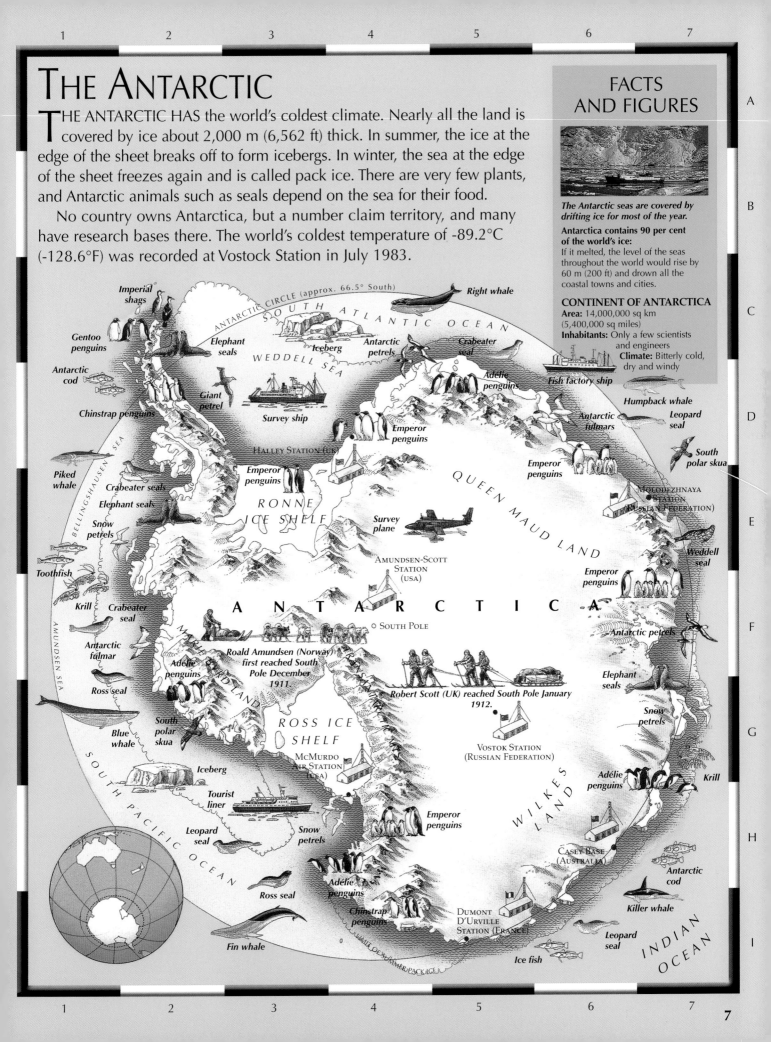

THE ANTARCTIC

THE ANTARCTIC HAS the world's coldest climate. Nearly all the land is covered by ice about 2,000 m (6,562 ft) thick. In summer, the ice at the edge of the sheet breaks off to form icebergs. In winter, the sea at the edge of the sheet freezes again and is called pack ice. There are very few plants, and Antarctic animals such as seals depend on the sea for their food.

No country owns Antarctica, but a number claim territory, and many have research bases there. The world's coldest temperature of -89.2°C (-128.6°F) was recorded at Vostock Station in July 1983.

FACTS AND FIGURES

The Antarctic seas are covered by drifting ice for most of the year.

Antarctica contains 90 per cent of the world's ice: If it melted, the level of the seas throughout the world would rise by 60 m (200 ft) and drown all the coastal towns and cities.

CONTINENT OF ANTARCTICA
Area: 14,000,000 sq km (5,400,000 sq miles)
Inhabitants: Only a few scientists and engineers
Climate: Bitterly cold, dry and windy

ANTARCTIC CIRCLE (approx. 66.5° South)

SOUTH ATLANTIC OCEAN

Imperial shags

Gentoo penguins

Antarctic cod

Chinstrap penguins

Elephant seals

Iceberg

WEDDELL SEA

Antarctic petrels

Crabeater seal

Right whale

Adélie penguins

Fish factory ship

Humpback whale

Antarctic fulmars

Leopard seal

South polar skua

Giant petrel

Survey ship

Emperor penguins

HALLEY STATION (UK)

Emperor penguins

Piked whale

Crabeater seals

Elephant seals

RONNE ICE SHELF

Survey plane

QUEEN MAUD LAND

Emperor penguins

MOLODEZHNAYA STATION (RUSSIAN FEDERATION)

BELLINGSHAUSEN SEA

Snow petrels

AMUNDSEN-SCOTT STATION (USA)

Weddell seal

Toothfish

Krill

Crabeater seal

Antarctic fulmar

A N T A R C T I C A

Emperor penguins

AMUNDSEN SEA

Ross seal

Adélie penguins

MARIE BYRD LAND

○ SOUTH POLE

Roald Amundsen (Norway) first reached South Pole December 1911.

Antarctic petrels

TRANSANTARCTIC MTNS

Robert Scott (UK) reached South Pole January 1912.

Elephant seals

Blue whale

South polar skua

ROSS ICE SHELF

VOSTOK STATION (RUSSIAN FEDERATION)

Snow petrels

Iceberg

McMURDO AIR STATION (USA)

WILKES LAND

Adélie penguins

Krill

SOUTH PACIFIC OCEAN

Tourist liner

Leopard seal

Snow petrels

Emperor penguins

CASEY BASE (AUSTRALIA)

Antarctic cod

Ross seal

Adélie penguins

Chinstrap penguins

DUMONT D'URVILLE STATION (FRANCE)

Killer whale

Fin whale

LIMIT OF SUMMER PACK ICE

Ice fish

Leopard seal

INDIAN OCEAN

THE BRITISH ISLES

THE BRITISH ISLES lie off the northwest coast of Europe. They consist of two large islands – Britain and Ireland – surrounded by smaller ones. The British Isles are divided into two countries: the United Kingdom and Ireland. The United Kingdom (UK) is made up of England, Wales, Scotland, and Northern Ireland.

During the 18th and 19th centuries, the UK was the first country to undergo an industrial revolution. It became the world's leading manufacturing and trading nation and acquired a vast empire, including Canada, Australia, New Zealand, India, and much of Africa. During the 20th century, most of these colonies became independent, although they remain linked with the UK through the Commonwealth. Today, the United Kingdom is a member of the European Union.

Until the last century, all of Ireland was part of the UK. In 1921 southern Ireland, where most people are Roman Catholic, became an independent country, while the northern part of Ireland, where the people are mainly Protestant, remained British.

FACTS AND FIGURES

The mountainous area of Snowdonia, in northern Wales, is traditionally popular for hill walking and mountaineering.

Largest cities:
London (Eng), 7,522,600;
Birmingham (Eng), 2,284,093;
Manchester (Eng), 2,240,230.
Highest mountains:
Ben Nevis (Scot), 1,343 m
(4,406 ft); Snowdon (Wales),
1,085 m (3,560 ft).
Longest rivers:
Severn (Eng–Wales), 354 km
(220 miles); Thames (Eng),
346 km (215 miles).

The parish church is the traditional centre of English country town and village life.

UNITED KINGDOM
Capital: London
Area: 244,017 sq km
(94,215 sq miles)
Population: 59,700,000
Language: English
Religion: Christian
Currency: Pound sterling
Government: Constitutional Monarchy

ENGLAND
Capital: London
Area: 130,360 sq km
(50,332 sq miles)
Population: 48,471,200

NORTHERN IRELAND
Capital: Belfast
Area: 14,121 sq km (5,452 sq miles)
Population: 1,943,400

SCOTLAND
Capital: Edinburgh
Area: 78,769 sq km (30,412 sq miles)
Population: 5,448,600

WALES
Capital: Cardiff
Area: 20,767 sq km (8,018 sq miles)
Population: 3,136,800

FACTS AND FIGURES

Much of Ireland's wealth comes from farming.

Largest metropolitan areas:
Dublin, 1,186,159;
Cork, 190,384; Limerick, 91,186
Highest mountain:
Carrauntoohil, 1,038 m (3,415 ft)
Longest river:
Shannon, 386 km (240 miles)

IRELAND
Capital: Dublin
Area: 70,284 sq km
(27,136 sq miles)
Population: 4,100,000
Languages: English, Irish
Religion: Christian
Currency: Euro
Government: Multiparty Republic

Crofting (farming)

Lerwick

SHETLAND ISLANDS

Pilchards

Seals

Cod

Haddock

ORKNEY ISLANDS

UNITED KINGDOM

Fish packing

Aberdeen

Oil rig

Fishing trawler

Highland dress

Whisky

BALMORAL CASTLE

BEN NEVIS 1,343 M

Machinery

Edinburgh

Red deer

Sheep

LOCH NESS MONSTER

LOCH LOMOND

EDINBURGH CASTLE

Glasgow

Golf

Sheep

ISLE OF LEWIS

Harris tweed

SCOTLAND

Salmon

ISLE OF MULL

SKYE

ISLE OF ARRAN

NORTH UIST

SOUTH UIST

OUTER HEBRIDES

Highland cattle

ISLAY

GIANT'S CAUSEWAY

Londonderry

MAP QUIZ

- Where was the poet and playwright William Shakespeare born?
- St George's Channel runs between which two countries?
- What river runs through Nottingham?
- The Vikings sailed to Ireland in wooden ships. Which Northern Irish city is famous for shipbuilding today?
- Name the two countries divided by Hadrian's wall, built by Roman soldiers.
- Can you find two castles in Scotland?
- Which British island plays host to an annual motorbike race?
- Which woollen fabric is woven on the Isle of Lewis in the Outer Hebrides?

FRANCE

FRANCE, ONE OF Europe's major farming and industrial nations, is famous for food and wine. The landscape varies dramatically from region to region and includes hot, dry areas, farmland, mountains, and forests.

France has always been powerful in Europe. In 1789 the people overthrew the king, Louis XVI, during what was later called the French Revolution. After the revolution, Napoleon, a general in the army, crowned himself Emperor. He went on to conquer most of Europe, but was defeated by the English at the Battle of Waterloo in 1815.

Today, France is a leading manufacturing country, with iron, steel, chemical, car, aeroplane, and textile industries. France is rich in farmland, and its major crops include oats, barley, wheat, flax, sugar beet, and grapes. Dairy farming is widespread and French farmers produce over 700 different types of cheese.

In terms of tourism, there are many coastal resorts, and the mountains are popular for winter sports.

MAP QUIZ

- On which river would you find the town of Arles, with its Roman Amphitheatre?

- The Pyrenees separate France from what other country?

- Name the widely used condiment associated with the city of Dijon.

- Which famous sparkling wine comes from northeastern France?

- Can you find the site of thousands of prehistoric standing stones?

- Which city on the edge of the Massif Central is best known for its porcelain industry?

- On which sea are the resort towns of Nice and Cannes?

- A winding river runs through the centre of Paris. Can you name it?

- Pigs are used to hunt for a rare edible fungus. What is it?

- Which city is a natural harbour at the mouth of the Seine river?

FACTS AND FIGURES

Amboise is one of the many historic towns along the River Loire.

Highest mountains:
Mont Blanc, 4,807 m (15,770 ft);
Les Ecrins, 4,103 m (13,461 ft);
Pic de Vignemale, 3,298 m (10,820 ft); Mont Dore, 1,886 m (6,188 ft).
Longest rivers:
Loire, 1,005 km (625 miles);
Rhône-Saône, 812 km (505 miles);
Seine, 775 km (481 miles).
Largest cities:
Paris, 9,930,100; Lyon, 1,783,400;
Marseille, 1,605,000; Bordeaux, 1,200,000; Lille, 1,000,900.

The high-speed TGV train, which runs between Paris and Lyon.

FRANCE
Capital: Paris
Area: 551,500 sq km (212,936 sq miles)
Population: 60,500,000
Language: French
Religion: Christian
Currency: Euro
MONACO
Capital: Monaco
Area: 1.6 sq km (0.6 sq miles)
Population: 32,000
Language: French
Religion: Christian
Currency: Euro

Sunflowers are grown all over southern France.

MONACO

CORSICA (France)
Bastia
CORSICA
Tourism
Ajaccio
Tourism

BELGIUM
GERMANY
LUXEMBOURG
SWITZERLAND
ITALY
Dunkirk
Lille
Calais
WORLD WAR I MEMORIAL (VIMY)
AMIENS CATHEDRAL
Beef cattle
Fashion design
CHÂTEAU BAS (SEDAN)
Reims
Coal
Coal
Wine
Metz
Potatoes
Strasbourg
Nancy
Storks
PARIS
CHÂTEAU DE PIERREFONDS
Champagne
Wheat
Seine
Wild boar
Pigs
Vosges
Mulhouse
CHARTRES CATHEDRAL
Orléans
Wine
Mustard
CHAPEL OF NOTRE DAME DU HAUT (RONCHAMP)
SAINTE MADELEINE (VÉZELAY)
Dijon
Beaune
Wine
Deer
JURA
CHÂTEAUNEUF (NIÈVRE)
Loire
Saône
Mâcon
Rhône
MONT BLANC 4,807 M
Porcelain
NCE
TGV high-speed train
Hunting for truffles
Clermont-Ferrand
Lyon
St Etienne
Skiing
ALPS
MASSIF CENTRAL
CHAPEL OF ST MICHEL D'AIGUILHE (LE PUY)
Grenoble
Mountain climbing
CÉVENNES
Rhône
Wine
Chamois (type of goat)
Sheep
Snails
VALENTRÉ (CAHORS)
Aircraft industry
Olives
Tourism
MONACO
Nice
Montpellier
AMPHITHEATRE AT ARLES
Lavender
Cannes
Tourism
WALLED TOWN (CARCASSONNE)
Marseille
Toulon
Tourism
Tourism
Fishing
Flamingos
Warship
Sailing
MEDITERRANEAN SEA
FURNACE (ODEILLO)
Wine
Sardines

BELGIUM, THE NETHERLANDS, AND LUXEMBOURG

BELGIUM, THE NETHERLANDS, and Luxembourg are called the "Low Countries" because they lie on the flat, low North European Plain. Almost half the Netherlands is below sea level. The saying, "God made the world, but the Dutch made the Netherlands", refers to the land they reclaimed from the sea. These areas, called polders, were drained, then protected from floods with walls, or dykes.

Belgium, the Netherlands, and Luxembourg are often called "Benelux", a short version of their names. These small countries have large populations: the Netherlands has one of the highest concentrations of people in Europe – an average of 480 in each square kilometre (1,245 per square mile). All three countries are industrial, but farming, fishing and tourism are also important. Belgium and the Netherlands have been trading nations for centuries, and today, Antwerp and Rotterdam are the two busiest ports in Europe.

The Benelux countries are part of the European Union based in Brussels. Luxembourg is a centre for European organizations, while the International Courts of Justice are situated at The Hague.

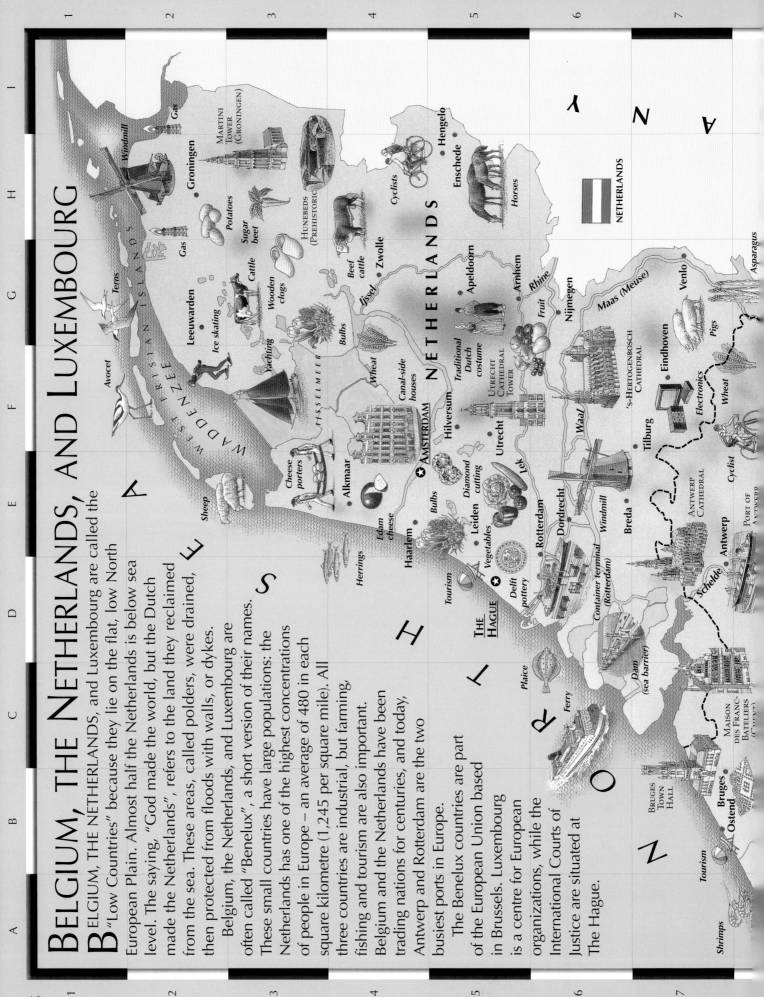

NETHERLANDS

MAP QUIZ

- Which country has the same name as its capital city?

- What modern Dutch city is famous for the manufacture of electronic equipment and appliances?

- Where would you find an international centre for the cutting and selling of diamonds?

- The Ardennes Mountains completely cover one of the Benelux countries. Which one is it?

- Name the Belgian city known for both its medieval stone buildings and the exquisite lace produced there.

- Some of the finest chocolate in the world is exported from this region. Which country is responsible?

- Can you find the headquarters of the European Union?

- What pretty blue-and-white pottery has been manufactured in the Netherlands for hundreds of years?

FACTS AND FIGURES

The historic Belgian city of Bruges is famous for its lace.

Highest mountain:
Mt Botrange (Belg), 694 m (2,277 ft).

Lowest point:
Prins Alexander Polder (Neth), 6.7 m (22 ft) below sea level.

Largest cities:
Amsterdam (Neth) 1,468,122;
Rotterdam (Neth), 1,069,400;
Brussels (Belg), 1,031,215;
The Hague (Neth), 694,400.

BELGIUM
Capital: Brussels
Area: 30,514 sq km (11,781 sq miles)
Population: 10,400,000
Languages: French, Dutch, some German
Religion: Christian
Currency: Euro

LUXEMBOURG
Capital: Luxembourg
Area: 2,586 sq km (998 sq miles)
Population: 465,000
Languages: Letzeburgesch, French, German
Religion: Christian
Currencies: Euro

NETHERLANDS
Capital: Amsterdam
Seat of government: The Hague
Area: 40,844 sq km (15,770 sq miles)
Population: 16,300,000
Language: Dutch
Religion: Christian
Currency: Euro

Rotterdam in the Netherlands is a major international port.

SCANDINAVIA

SCANDINAVIA CONSISTS OF Denmark, Norway, Sweden, and Finland in northern Europe, and the island of Iceland in the North Atlantic. Denmark is low lying farmland, whereas most of Norway is mountainous with coastal bays called fjords. Finland is full of forests and lakes, while Sweden has a varied landscape that includes forest, farmland, mountains and lakes. Central Iceland is a plateau of volcanoes, lava fields and glaciers, so most people live near the coast. Scandinavia has important natural resources, including timber, fish, iron ore and oil and natural gas in the North Sea. Today, the Scandinavian countries are all industrial, and their people enjoy a high standard of living.

MAP QUIZ

- Lego building blocks were invented in which Scandinavian country, where there is a theme park dedicated to them?

- Where would you see the statue of the Little Mermaid?

- Can you identify two Scandinavian countries that have large paper-making industries?

- Name a region where you can find reindeer like the ones associated with the legend of Father Christmas.

- In which country are Volvo cars manufactured?

- A large mountain range runs along the border between Norway and Sweden. What is it called?

NORWAY

NORWEGIAN SEA

ATLANTIC OCEAN

Fishing trawler

Salmon

Coastal express

Trondheim

Skiing

Wolverine

STAVE CHURCH (BORGUND)

GALDHØPIGGEN 2,460 M

Mountain climbing

Bergen

CITY HALL (OSLO)

Ski jumping

Electric power

OSLO

Paper

Stavanger

Folk costume

Karlsta

LAKE VÄNERI

Sheep

Oil and gas

Herrings

SKAGERRAK

STATUE OF POSEIDON

Borås

I VÄ

Gothenburg

Volvo ca

Dairy cattle

KRONBORG C HELSING

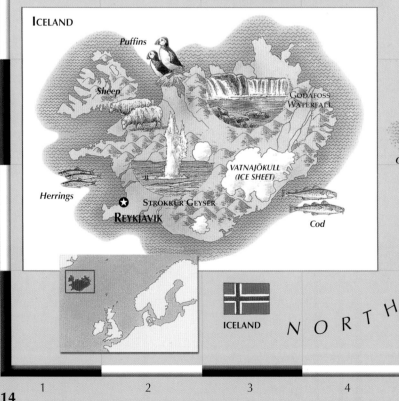

ICELAND

Puffins

Sheep

GODAFOSS WATERFALL

VATNAJÖKULL (ICE SHEET)

Herrings

STRÖKKUR GEYSER

REYKJAVIK

Cod

NORTH SEA

LEGOLAND

Aarhus

DENMARK

Esbjerg

COPENHAGEN

Malmö

Pigs

LITTLE MERMAID STATUE (COPENHAGEN)

GERMANY

ICELAND

DENMARK

NORTH CAPE

BARENTS SEA

Fishing trawler

Cod

Tromso

LOFOTEN ISLANDS

Puffins

Narvik

Iron ore

Salmon

Elk

Lynx

Cross-country skiing

Norway spruce

Umeå

Salmon

Folk costume

Model horse (Dalarna)

Herrings

DROTTNINGHOLM PALACE

bro

Uppsala

STOCKHOLM

City Hall (STOCKHOLM)

Rune stone (ancient inscription)

GOTLAND

OLAND

Guillemots

SWEDEN

KJØLEN MTS

VESTERALEN

LAPLAND

Reindeer

Sami (Lapps)

Wolves

Birch tree

FINLAND

Sailing

Oulu

Sauna

Furs

Scots pine

TAMPERE CATHEDRAL

Paper

Tampere

Lahti

Potatoes

Turku

ALAND ISLANDS

HELSINKI

HELSINKI RAILWAY STATION

Trout

GULF OF BOTHNIA

GULF OF FINLAND

Ice-breaker ship

ESTONIA

BALTIC SEA

LATVIA

RUSSIAN FEDERATION

0   50   100   150   200   250 Kilometres
0   50   100   150 Miles

FACTS AND FIGURES

Scandinavia's forests support large timber and paper industries.

Highest mountain:
Galdhøpiggen (Norway), 2,469 m (8,100 ft).

Largest lake:
Lake Vänern (Sweden), 5,580 sq km (2,155 sq miles).

Largest cities:
Copenhagen (Denmark), 1,145,804; Stockholm (Sweden), 1,949,516; Helsinki (Finland), 1,293,262; Oslo (Norway) 839,423; Gothenborg (Sweden) 890,956.

Copenhagen has been a port and trading centre since the Middle Ages.

DENMARK
Capital: Copenhagen
Area: 43,077 sq km (16,632 sq miles)
Population: 5,400,000
Language: Danish
Religion: Christian
Currency: Danish krone
Government: Constitutional Monarchy

FINLAND
Capital: Helsinki
Area: 338,127 sq km (130,551 sq miles)
Population: 5,200,000
Languages: Finnish, Swedish, Lappish
Religion: Christian
Currency: Euro
Government: Multiparty Republic

ICELAND
Capital: Reykjavik
Area: 103,000 sq km (39,768 sq miles)
Population: 295,000
Language: Icelandic
Religion: Christian
Currency: Icelandic krona
Government: Constitutional Republic

NORWAY
Capital: Oslo
Area: 323,895 sq km (125,056 sq miles)
Population: 4,600,000
Languages: Norwegian, Lappish
Religion: Christian
Currency: Norwegian krona
Government: Constitutional Monarchy

SWEDEN
Capital: Stockholm
Area: 440,945 sq km (170,250 sq miles)
Population: 9,000,000
Languages: Swedish, Lappish
Religion: Christian
Currency: Swedish krone
Government: Constitutional Monarchy

GERMANY, AUSTRIA, AND SWITZERLAND

THE LANDSCAPE IN this region is crossed by two of Europe's longest rivers: the Rhine, flowing north to the North Sea, and the Danube, flowing east to the Black Sea.

For hundreds of years, the area now called Germany consisted of small independent states, which were first united in 1871. Germany rapidly became an important power, but after World War II, the country was split into two parts: the Federal Republic of Germany (West Germany) and the communist German Democratic Republic (East Germany). This split lasted for over 40 years. The two German states were reunited in 1990, following the collapse of communism in East Germany. Today, Germany is the wealthiest country in Europe and one of the world's foremost industrial nations.

To the south lie the mountainous countries of Austria and Switzerland, which both rely heavily on tourism. Switzerland is famous for watches and scientific instruments, and it is also a major business centre. Becoming neutral in 1815, it has stayed out of every war affecting Europe since then. Austria is also neutral. The tiny country of Liechtenstein is only about 24 km (15 miles) long and 8 km (5 miles) wide.

| 0 | 50 | 100 | 150 | 200 | Kilometres |
| 0 | 25 | 50 | 75 | 100 | 125 | Miles |

The Alps

EIGER 3,970 M   MÖNCH 4,099 M   JUNGFRAU 4,158 M

The Alps are the longest and highest mountain range in western Europe. They stretch from southeastern France, through Italy, Switzerland, Austria, Slovenia, and Croatia – a distance of about 1,200 km (750 miles). People from around the world visit the Alps to take part in sports such as skiing and mountaineering.

NORTH SEA

DENMARK

Pigs
Sailing
Kiel
KIEL CANAL
Shipbuilding
Cod
Tourism
Lübeck
Hamburg
Elbe
Electronics
Bremerhaven
Bremen
Potatoes
Dairy cattle
BREMEN CATHEDRAL
Weser
Wheat
Beef cattle
LÜNEBURG HEATH
Hannover
HANNOVER TOWN HA
Iron and steel
Sausages
Coal
Lippe
Machinery
Ruhr
Essen
Dortmund
Volkswagen cars
Düsseldorf
COLOGNE CATHEDRAL
Kassel
Sugar beet
Chemicals
Cologne
G E R M A N
Bonn
Potatoes
Erfu
Strip-mining coal
Frankfurt skyline
BEETHOVEN'S BIRTHPLACE
Wiesbaden
Wheat
THE LORELEI ROCK
Frankfurt am Main
Lebkuch biscuit
Mainz
Main
Wine
Wine
Mannheim
Nurem
Saarbrücken
Coal
ROTHENBURG TOWN HALL
Traditional Bavarian costume
F R A N C E
Stuttgart
Cuckoo clocks
Mercedes-Benz cars
ULM CATHEDRAL
Danu
LIECHTENSTEIN
NEUSCHWANSTEIN CASTLE
Rhine
Freiburg im Breisgau
HOHENZOLLERN CASTLE
SWITZERLAND
Watches
LAKE CONSTANCE
Basel
Traditional Swiss costume
VADUZ
Innsbr
LIECHTENSTEIN
Gruyère cheese
Dairy cattle
Zurich
BERN ✪
S W I T Z E R L A N D
A
Lausanne
Marm
LAKE GENEVA
Chocolate
Geneva
Skiing
Alpine horns
I T
MATTERHORN 4,478 M

THE NETHERLANDS
BELGIUM
LUXEMBOURG

Shipbuilding

BALTIC SEA

RÜGEN

Rostock

Storks

Sheep

werin

BRANDENBURG GATE

GERMANY

Sugar beet

Dairy cattle

Machinery

P O L A N D

★ **BERLIN**

Potsdam

Magdeburg

Pigs

Poultry

Halle

Elbe

Textiles
Dresden

ZWINGER PALACE

Leipzig

p—ing —al

Chemnitz

Zwickau

Iron and steel

C Z E C H R E P U B L I C

REGENSBURG CATHEDRAL

Regensburg

Cakes

Beer

Sugar beet

Electronics

munich

Linz

Lipizzaner horses

Danube

VIENNA OPERA HOUSE

VIENNA ★

Iron and steel

S L O V A K I A

Dairy cattle

HOHENSALZBURG CASTLE

Salzburg

MOZART'S BIRTHPLACE

iolins

A U S T R I A

Great white heron

MARIA-HILF-KIRCHE (GRAZ)

Graz

S

Edelweiss

Skiing

AUSTRIA

Chamois (type of goat)

Mountain climbing

H U N G A R Y

L Y

S L O V E N I A

FACTS AND FIGURES

Vienna's Belvedere Castle was built for the Habsburg family.

Longest rivers:
Danube, 2,858 km (1,776 miles); Rhine, 1,320 km (820 miles).

Largest lakes:
Lake Geneva (Switz-Fr), 580 sq km (224 sq miles); Lake Constance (Ger-Switz-Aust), 539 sq km (208 sq miles).

Largest cities:
Berlin (Ger), 3,700,000; Hamburg (Ger), 1,766,156; Vienna (Aust), 1,678,435; Munich (Ger), 1,348,650; Zurich (Switz), 1,007,972;, Cologne (Ger), 991,395; Frankfurt (Ger), 667,598; Essen (Ger), 581,406.

World's tallest spire:
The cathedral of Ulm in Germany has the world's tallest church spire. It is 161-m (528 ft) high.

Busiest canal:
Germany's Kiel Canal is the busiest in the world. Every year, about 45,000 ships use it to pass between the North Sea and the Baltic Sea.

World's biggest roof:
The glass roof over the Olympic Stadium in Munich measures 85,000 sq m (914,940 sq ft).

Cows grazing in the Alps give milk for Swiss chocolate.

AUSTRIA
Capital: Vienna
Area: 83,853 sq km (32,375 sq miles)
Population: 8,200,000
Language: German
Religion: Christian
Currency: Euro
Government: Multiparty Republic

GERMANY
Capital: Berlin
Area: 356,910 sq km (137,804 sq miles)
Population: 82,700,000
Language: German
Religion: Christian
Currency: Euro
Government: Multiparty Republic

LIECHTENSTEIN
Capital: Vaduz
Area: 160 sq km (62 sq miles)
Population: 33,700
Language: German
Religion: Christian
Currency: Swiss franc
Government: Constititional Monarchy

SWITZERLAND
Capital: Bern
Area: 41,293 sq km (15,943 sq miles)
Population: 7,300,000
Languages: German, French, Italian
Religion: Christian
Currency: Swiss franc
Government: Federal Republic

MAP QUIZ

- What mountain range extends across Germany, Austria and Switzerland?

- By which river would you find the Lorelei Rock, where a legendary water nymph lured sailors to their death?

- The birthplace of Wolfgang Amadeus Mozart is now the home of an important music festival. Which city is it?

- Name two important car manufacturers that are based in Germany.

- Which city is famous for its Opera House, its rich cakes and its elegant Lipizzaner horses?

- In which country would you be able to hear the distinctive sound of alpine horns?

- List four German cities that have beautiful old cathedrals shown on the map.

- Identify the country most closely associated with the white edelweiss flower.

- Where is the huge Matterhorn mountain?

SPAIN AND PORTUGAL

THE COUNTRIES OF Spain and Portugal occupy the Iberian Peninsula, which also contains the tiny independent state of Andorra and the British colony of Gibraltar.

Over time, Spain and Portugal have been invaded by many peoples, including the Romans and the Moors – Arabs from North Africa who ruled much of Spain for hundreds of years. Both countries have a long history of exploration: Columbus sailed from Spain to America in 1492, and in 1497, the Portuguese adventurer Vasco da Gama sailed around Africa to India for the first time. Settlers followed explorers, and by the 16th century Spain and Portugal had empires in North and South America, Asia, and Africa.

Today, many people make their living from farming or fishing, or in industry. Tourism is a major source of wealth in both countries.

MAP QUIZ

- Lisbon, the Portuguese capital, lies at the mouth of which river?

- Where would you go to see the annual event known as Running with the Bulls?

- In which Spanish city would you find the House of Shells?

- Portugal and Spain each have their own fortified wine. Can you name them?

- Find the Spanish town that is known for its prehistoric cave paintings.

- Which city, also famous for guitars, has a Roman aqueduct?

BAY OF BISC

Shellfish
Fish packing
Iron and steel
Gijón
Santan
La Coruña
Oviedo
Apples
Horses
CATHEDRAL OF SANTIAGO DE COMPOSTELA
Brown bear
Coal
CAVE PAINTING (ALTAMIRA)
Santiago
León
Cattle
Vigo
Potatoes
LEÓN CATHEDRAL
Wheat
Fish packing
Minho
Textiles
Egyptian vulture
Valladolid
S
P
Braga
Anchovies
Cattle
Porto
DOURO
Salamanca
Segovia
Port wine
HOUSE OF SHELLS (SALAMANCA)
Ávila
Transporting port wine
Potatoes
Fish packing
Rugs
STATUE OF PIZARRO (TRUJILLO)
Mackerel
Coimbra
PORTUGAL
Tol
Pilchards
Tagus
ATLANTIC OCEAN
PORTUGAL
Olive trees
Wine
ROMAN THEATRE
TOLEDO CATHEDRAL
BELÉM TOWER
Tagus
ROMAN TEMPLE (ÉVORA)
Mérida
Manchego cheese
LISBON ★
Badajoz
Guadiana
Sheep
Setúbal
CÓRDOBA MOSQUE
Fish packing
Windmill
Bulls
SEVILLE CATHEDRAL
Córdoba
Guadalquivir
Sardines
Cork oak
Citrus fruits
Guadiana
Seville
Holy week procession (Seville)
Wine
Tourism
Tourism
Pardel lynx
Faro
Sherry
Lobster
Jeréz de la Frontera
Má
Cádiz
ROCK OF GIBRALTAR
GIBRALTAR (UK)
STRAIT OF GIBRALTAR
Ceuta (Spain)
Tuna

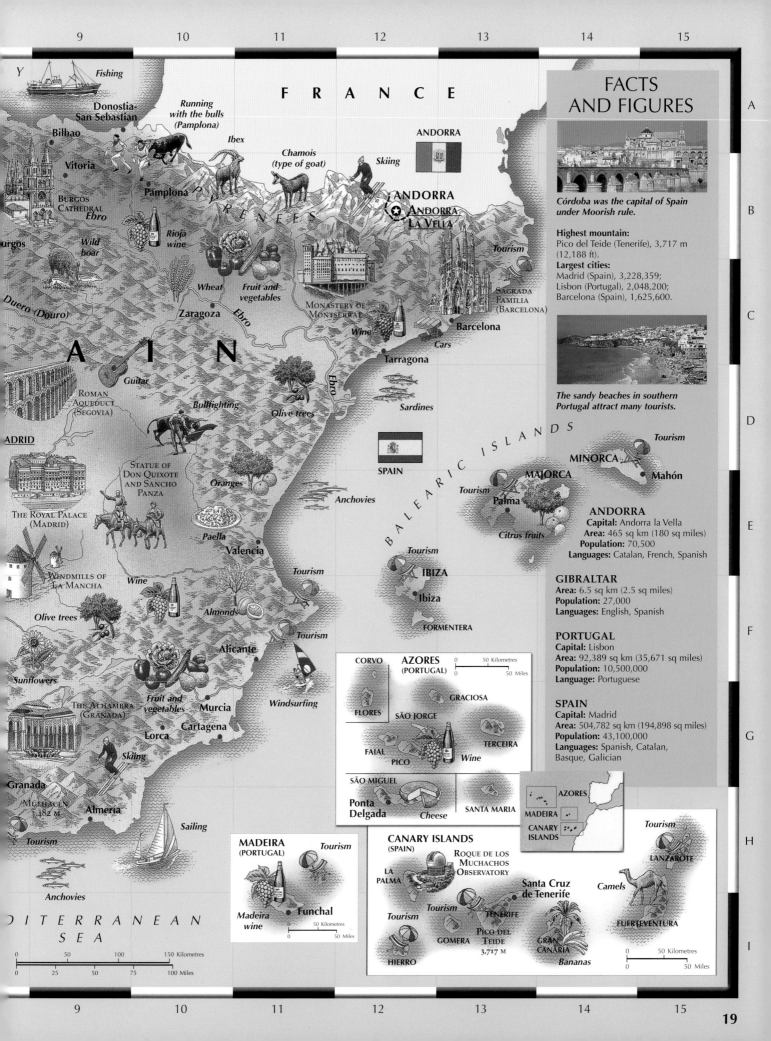

FRANCE

ANDORRA

Y

Fishing

Donostia-San Sebastián

Bilbao

Vitoria

Running with the bulls (Pamplona)

Ibex

Chamois (type of goat)

Skiing

ANDORRA
Andorra la Vella

Burgos Cathedral

Pamplona

P Y R E N E E S

Ebro

urgos

Burgos

Wild boar

Rioja wine

Wheat

Fruit and vegetables

MONASTERY OF MONTSERRAT

Tourism

SAGRADA FAMILIA (BARCELONA)

Duero (Douro)

Zaragoza

Ebro

Wine

Barcelona

A   I   N

Guitar

ROMAN AQUEDUCT (SEGOVIA)

Bullfighting

Olive trees

Ebro

Tarragona

Cars

Sardines

SPAIN

B A L E A R I C   I S L A N D S

ADRID

MADRID

THE ROYAL PALACE (MADRID)

STATUE OF DON QUIXOTE AND SANCHO PANZA

Oranges

Anchovies

MINORCA

Mahón

Tourism

MAJORCA

Palma

Tourism

WINDMILLS OF LA MANCHA

Paella

Valencia

Tourism

Citrus fruits

Wine

Almonds

Tourism

IBIZA

Ibiza

Olive trees

Fruit and vegetables

Alicante

Tourism

FORMENTERA

Sunflowers

THE ALHAMBRA (GRANADA)

Murcia

Windsurfing

Lorca

Cartagena

Skiing

Granada

MULHACÉN 3,482 M

Almería

Sailing

Tourism

Anchovies

M E D I T E R R A N E A N   S E A

0 50 100 150 Kilometres
0 25 50 75 100 Miles

FACTS AND FIGURES

Córdoba was the capital of Spain under Moorish rule.

Highest mountain:
Pico del Teide (Tenerife), 3,717 m (12,188 ft).
Largest cities:
Madrid (Spain), 3,228,359;
Lisbon (Portugal), 2,048,200;
Barcelona (Spain), 1,625,600.

The sandy beaches in southern Portugal attract many tourists.

ANDORRA
Capital: Andorra la Vella
Area: 465 sq km (180 sq miles)
Population: 70,500
Languages: Catalan, French, Spanish

GIBRALTAR
Area: 6.5 sq km (2.5 sq miles)
Population: 27,000
Languages: English, Spanish

PORTUGAL
Capital: Lisbon
Area: 92,389 sq km (35,671 sq miles)
Population: 10,500,000
Language: Portuguese

SPAIN
Capital: Madrid
Area: 504,782 sq km (194,898 sq miles)
Population: 43,100,000
Languages: Spanish, Catalan, Basque, Galician

AZORES (PORTUGAL)

CORVO

FLORES

GRACIOSA

SÃO JORGE

FAIAL

PICO

TERCEIRA

Wine

SÃO MIGUEL

Ponta Delgada

Cheese

SANTA MARIA

0 50 Kilometres
0 50 Miles

AZORES

MADEIRA

CANARY ISLANDS

MADEIRA (PORTUGAL)

Tourism

Madeira wine

Funchal

0 50 Kilometres
0 50 Miles

CANARY ISLANDS (SPAIN)

ROQUE DE LOS MUCHACHOS OBSERVATORY

LA PALMA

Tourism

Santa Cruz de Tenerife

Tourism

TENERIFE

Tourism

GOMERA

PICO DEL TEIDE 3,717 M

GRAN CANARIA

HIERRO

Bananas

Tourism

LANZAROTE

Camels

FUERTEVENTURA

0 50 Kilometres
0 50 Miles

19

ITALY

THE EASILY RECOGNIZABLE boot shape of Italy is a 800-km (500-mile) long peninsula that stretches south into the Mediterranean Sea. Most of the country is mountainous or hilly, and in the north, the Alps form a barrier between Italy and the rest of Europe. Running down the spine of the country are the Apennines, rugged mountains dotted with villages and towns that haven't changed for centuries. The Mediterranean islands of Sicily and Sardinia are also part of Italy.

Modern Italy, with Rome as its capital, only came into existence in 1870. Before then, the area was a patchwork of independent city states, and these states can still be seen today in Italy's 20 "regions". Two have remained independent – the Vatican City in Rome and the Republic of San Marino in northeastern Italy.

In Roman times, the Italian peninsula was the centre of a great empire, and the remains of Roman roads and buildings can still be seen. In the 14th–16th centuries, Italy was the centre of an important artistic movement called the Renaissance. Many beautiful paintings, sculptures, buildings, and poems were produced here, and among Italy's most famous Renaissance artists and writers were Michelangelo, Leonardo da Vinci, Raphael, and Dante. Today, millions of tourists each year visit Italy's ancient cities and art treasures.

Modern Italy has large steel, chemical, textile, and car industries, and farming is still important: wheat, corn, rice, grapes and olives are the main crops. Fishing plays a part too, with fresh seafood coming into many small coastal ports.

FACTS AND FIGURES

Venice is built on islands and has many canals in place of streets.

ITALY
Capital: Rome
Area: 301,268 sq km (116,320 sq miles)
Population: 58,100,000
Language: Italian
Religion: Christian
Currency: Euro
Government: Multiparty Republic

MALTA
Capital: Valletta
Area: 316 sq km (122 sq miles)
Population: 402,000
Languages: Maltese, English
Religion: Christian
Currency: Euro
Government: Multiparty Republic

SAN MARINO
Capital: San Marino
Area: 61 sq km (23 sq miles)
Population: 28,800
Language: Italian
Religion: Christian
Currency: Euro
Government: Multiparty Republic

VATICAN CITY
Area: 0.44 sq km (0.17 sq miles)
Population: 1,000

Highest mountains:
Mont Blanc (It-Fr), 4,807 m (15,770 ft); Monte Rosa (It-Switz), 4,634 m (15,203 ft).
Longest river:
Po, 672 km (418 miles).
Largest lakes:
Lake Garda, 370 sq km (143 sq miles); Lake Maggiore, 212 sq km (82 sq miles); Lake Como, 145 sq km (55 sq miles).
Largest cities:
Rome, 2,705,603; Milan, 1,305,591; Naples, 1,046,987; Turin, 921,485.

A horse race called the Palio takes place in Siena each year.

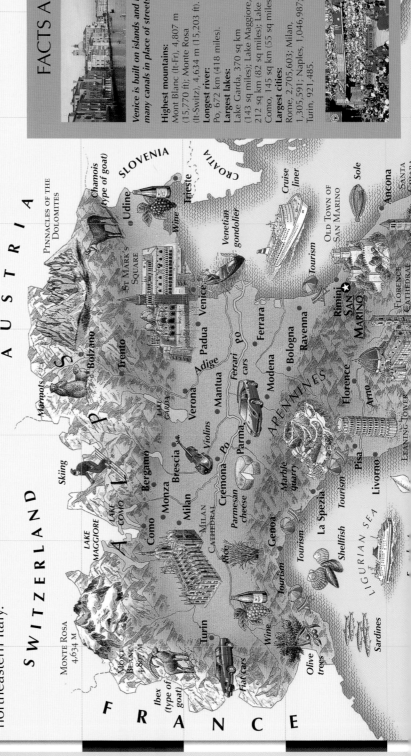

SWITZERLAND

AUSTRIA

SLOVENIA

CROATIA

FRANCE

A L P S

APENNINES

LIGURIAN SEA

MONTE ROSA 4,634 M

MONT BLANC 4,807 M

Ibex (type of goat)

Skiing

Marmots

PINNACLES OF THE DOLOMITES

Chamois (type of goat)

Turin

Fiat cars

Wine

Olive trees

Sardines

Tourism

Tourism

Tourism

Rice

Violins

Monza

Bergamo

Brescia

Como

Milan

MILAN CATHEDRAL

LAKE MAGGIORE

LAKE COMO

LAKE GARDA

Cremona

Parmesan cheese

Parma

Po

Bolzano

Trento

Verona

Mantua

Ferrari cars

Adige

Modena

Bologna

Ferrara

Ravenna

Padua

Venice

ST MARK'S SQUARE

Venetian gondolier

Udine

Trieste

Wine

Cruise liner

Genoa

La Spezia

Livorno

Pisa

LEANING TOWER

Florence

FLORENCE CATHEDRAL

Arno

Marble quarry

Shellfish

Tourism

Tourism

Rimini

SAN MARINO

OLD TOWN OF SAN MARINO

Tourism

Ancona

SANTA CHIARA

Sole

ADRIATIC SEA

IONIAN SEA

MEDITERRANEAN SEA

TYRRHENIAN SEA

ITALY

APENNINES

ROME

VATICAN CITY

Tiber

THE COLOSSEUM (ROME)

VESUVIUS 1277 M

Wine

Palio

Pasta

Sea bream

Red mullet

Pescara

Tobacco

Almonds

Foggia

Salerno

Pizza

Naples

Shellfish

CAPRI

ISCHIA

Tourism

Prawns

Octopus

CASTEL DEL MONTE

Bari

Steel

Crabs

Wine

Brindisi

Taranto

Oysters

Citrus fruits

Olive trees

Goats

TEMPLE OF NEPTUNE

Garfish

Anchovies

Crotone

BRONZES OF RIACE

Reggio di Calabria

Tourism

STROMBOLI

AEOLIAN ISLANDS

Swordfish

Messina

Mt ETNA 3323 M

Tourism

SICILY

Palermo

Citrus fruits

Agrigento

Carob tree

Syracuse

Ragusa

TEMPLE OF CASTOR AND POLLOX

Wine

USTICA

PANTELLERIA

GOZO

VALLETTA

MALTA

SARDINIA

CORSICA

GIGLIO

ELBA

Ferry boat

Grey mullet

Scuba diving

Tourism

Tuna

Sardines

Goats and sheep

Olive trees

Citrus fruits

Wine

Cagliari

Tourism

Petro-chemicals

Crayfish

Sea bream

Wine

Tobacco

🟥⬜ MALTA	
⬜🟦 SAN MARINO	
VATICAN CITY	
🟩⬜🟥 ITALY	

MAP QUIZ

- Where would you find the live volcano of Mount Etna?

- Name the five seas that surround Italy.

- Which river runs through Florence?

- In what city are Fiat cars manufactured?

- Which Italian island gave its name to a small fish that lives in the surrounding waters?

- Gladiators once fought to the death in the Colosseum. Where is it?

- Which city in the Alps shares its name with the lake it lies on?

150 Kilometres

100 Miles

21

CENTRAL AND EASTERN EUROPE

THIS REGION HAS always been subject to change, and the borders have shifted many times. After World War II, all the countries apart from Greece became part of the "Eastern Bloc". They had communist regimes and ties with the former USSR. In recent years, however, many nations have established democratic governments with links to Western Europe.

The north of the region is dominated by Poland, which is rich in coal and copper, with large iron, steel, shipbuilding and textile industries. Farming is also important: the main crops are potatoes, wheat, and sugar beet.

To the south lie the Czech Republic and Slovakia, which until 1993 were one country – Czechoslovakia – with two peoples (Czechs and Slovaks) speaking different languages.

Below this is southeastern Europe: Greece, Albania, Bosnia and Herzegovina, Croatia, Serbia, Kosovo, Montenegro, Slovenia, Macedonia, Bulgaria, Romania, and Hungary. Many of these countries were only formed at the end of the two World Wars. More recently, the republics of Bosnia and Herzegovina, Croatia, Serbia, Kosovo, Montenegro, Macedonia and Slovenia emerged from the break up of the former Yugoslavia.

FACTS AND FIGURES

There are many picturesque towns along the Adriatic coast.

Largest cities:
Athens (Greece), 3,187,734;
Budapest (Hungary), 1,777,921
Longest river:
Danube, 2,858 km (1,776 miles).
Highest mountains:
Musala (Bulgaria), 2,925 m
(9,596 ft); Mt Olympus (Greece),
2,917 m (9,570 ft).

Many old buildings in Warsaw were rebuilt after World War II.

ALBANIA
Capital: Tirana
Area: 28,748 sq km (11,099 sq miles)
Population: 3,100,000

BOSNIA & HERZEGOVINA
Capital: Sarajevo
Area: 51,129 sq km (19,741 sq miles)

Map labels

LITHUANIA
RUSS. FED.
BELARUS
UKRAINE
BALTIC SEA
GERMANY
AUSTRIA

POLAND
HUNGARY
BULGARIA
ROMANIA
CZECH REPUBLIC
SLOVAKIA
SLOVENIA

European bison
Świeta Lipka Basilica
Bug
Palace of Culture
WARSAW
Lublin
Łódź
Sugar beet
Wheat
Vistula
Sheep
Skiing
Kielce
Kraków
Katowice
Iron and steel
Wrocław
Coal
Wałbrzych
Copper
Folk costume
Brno
Morava
Ostrava
BRATISLAVA
SLOVAKIA
Košice
CARPATHIAN MTS.
Bratislava Castle
PARLIAMENT BUILDINGS (BUDAPEST)
BUDAPEST
Debrecen
Chemicals
Spruce
Wild boar
Cattle
Wine
Skoda cars
Pilsen lager
CZECH REPUBLIC
PRAGUE
Cathedral of St Vitus
Machinery
Skiing
Wooden windmills
Szczecin
Oder
Shipbuilding
Potatoes
Tourism
Gdańsk
Chemicals
Bydgoszcz
Vistula
Poznań
Poznan Town Hall
Pigs
Masurian Lakes
Shipbuilding

400 Kilometres
250 Miles
0 50 100 150 200 300

Country Information

BULGARIA
Capital: Sofia
Area: 110,912 sq km (42,823 sq miles)
Population: 7,700,000

CROATIA
Capital: Zagreb
Area: 56,538 sq km (21,829 sq miles)
Population: 4,600,000

CZECH REPUBLIC
Capital: Prague
Area: 78,864 sq km (30,449 sq miles)
Population: 10,200,000

GREECE
Capital: Athens
Area: 131,990 sq km (50,961 sq miles)
Population: 11,100,000

HUNGARY
Capital: Budapest
Area: 93,032 sq km (35,919 sq miles)
Population: 10,100,000

KOSOVO
Capital: Pristina
Area: 10,800 sq km (4,200 sq miles)
Population: 1,900,000

MACEDONIA
Capital: Skopje
Area: 25,713 sq km (9,928 sq miles)
Population: 2,000,000

MONTENEGRO
Capital: Podgorica
Area: 13,812 sq km (5,300 sq miles)
Population: 620,000

POLAND
Capital: Warsaw
Area: 312,685 sq km (120,728 sq miles)
Population: 38,500,000

ROMANIA
Capital: Bucharest
Area: 237,500 sq km (91,699 sq miles)
Population: 21,700,000

SERBIA
Capital: Belgrade
Area: 77,561 sq km (29,900 sq miles)
Population: 7,800,000

SLOVAKIA
Capital: Bratislava
Area: 49,035 sq km (18,932 sq miles)
Population: 5,400,000

SLOVENIA
Capital: Ljubljana
Area: 20,251 sq km (7,819 sq miles)
Population: 2,000,000

Map Labels

Prut
MOLDOVA
Danube
BRAN CASTLE
TRIUMPHAL ARCH (BUCHAREST)
Constanţa
Tourism
BLACK SEA
Burgas
SEA OF MARMARA
ROMANIA
Braşov
Ploieşti
Oil
BUCHAREST
Sunflowers
Roses
Tobacco
TURKEY
Sibiu
TRANSYLVANIAN ALPS
Skiing
ALEXANDER NEVSKY CATHEDRAL
Sheep
Pilovdiv
BALKAN MOUNTAINS
BULGARIA
Grapes
Timişoara
Iron and steel
MUSALA 2,925 m
Textiles
MONASTERY
Rila
AEGEAN SEA
Sailing
Szeged
Textiles
Niš
SOFIA
Textiles
Thessaloniki
Olives
Octopus
Evzones (parliament guards)
ATHENS
Piraeus
BELGRADE
PRISTINA
SKOPJE
Skiing
Wheat
Novi Sad
Copper
SERBIA
KOSOVO (Disputed)
Iron and steel
MACEDONIA
LAKE PRESPA
Sheep and goats
Grapes
GREECE
RUINS OF DELPHI
Ferry
DODECANESE ISLANDS
Tourism
RHODES
Dolphins
Pigs
Danube
Brown bear
PODGORICA
LAKE OHRID
ALBANIA
Cotton
RUINS OF OLYMPIA
CRETE
Irákleio
RUINS OF KNOSSOS
Deer
Iron and steel
SARAJEVO
MONTENEGRO
TIRANA
Carpets
Sheep
Mt Olympus
Tobacco
IONIAN SEA
IONIAN ISLANDS
CORFU
Tourism
Cruise ship
GREECE
Drava
Sava
BOSNIA & HERZEGOVINA
CATHEDRAL OF ST STEPHEN (ZAGREB)
LAKE SCUTARI
ADRIATIC SEA
Tourism
DUBROVNIK WALLED TOWN
Split
ZAGREB
CROATIA
Shipbuilding
ROMAN AMPHITHEATRE (PULA)
ITALY
MEDITERRANEAN SEA

Flags: CROATIA, BOSNIA & HERZEGOVINA, SERBIA, KOSOVO, MACEDONIA, ALBANIA, MONTENEGRO

MAP QUIZ

- The goddess Athena gave her name to the Greek capital. What is it?
- On which island are the Ruins of Knossos?
- The walled town of Dubrovnik looks over which sea?
- Where can you see a Roman Amphitheatre?
- In which city is the Cathedral of St Vitus?
- Can you find a mountain range in Romania?
- The capital of Slovakia has its own castle. What is its name?
- Where are Skoda cars made?
- Name a monastery in Bulgaria.

NORTHERN EURASIA

This region spans two continents, Europe and Asia, separated by the Ural Mountains. Asia is bigger than Europe, taking up about 75 per cent of the land area, but only about 35 per cent of the people live there.

In the east lies Siberia, much of which is uninhabited wilderness. The climate there is extremely cold, and in winter the temperature falls below -45°C (-49°F), but this area is rich in gems and oil.

From 1922 to 1991, northern Eurasia was one vast country, called the Union of Soviet Socialist Republics, or USSR. The world's largest country, it was made up of 15 republics, each with a communist government. In 1991, the USSR split apart and all the republics became independent. The largest – the Russian Federation – remained dominant and drew many of the new nations into a Commonwealth of Independent States.

MAP QUIZ

- The Trans-Siberian Railway travels between which two cities?

- Name a type of Russian three-horse sledge.

- Which river runs through the city of Kiev and into the Black Sea?

- Can you find a precious gem that is mined in the Central Siberian Uplands?

- What do you call the painted Russian dolls that fit inside one another?

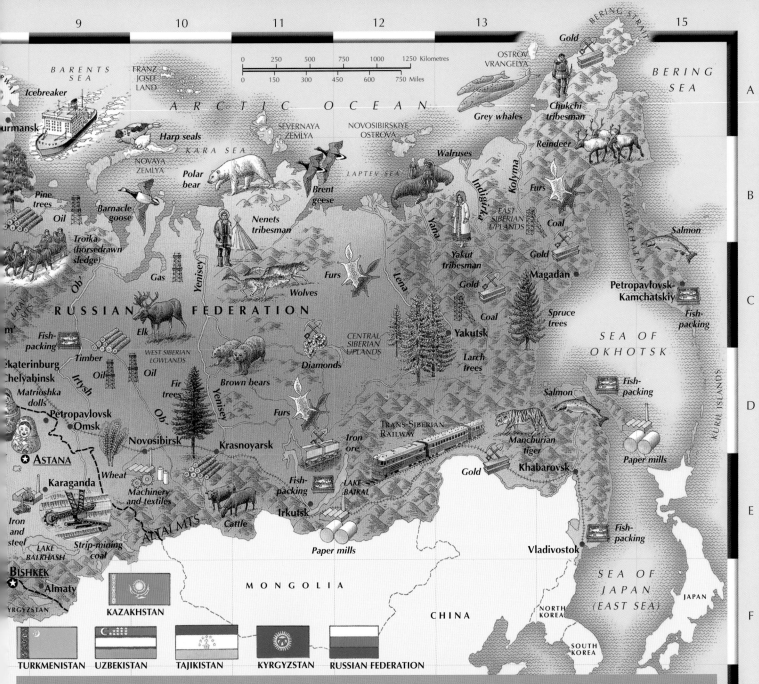

FACTS AND FIGURES

Largest lake:
Caspian Sea (the largest lake in the world) covers an area of 3,600,000 sq km (143,205 sq miles).

World's longest railway:
Trans-Siberian, Moscow to Nakhodka near Vladivostok, 9,438 km (5,864 miles).

ARMENIA
Capital: Yerevan
Area: 29,800 sq km (11,490 sq miles)
Population: 3,000,000
Languages: Armenian, Russian

AZERBAIJAN
Capital: Baku
Area: 86,600 sq km (33,340 sq miles)
Population: 8,400,000
Language: Azerbaijani

BELARUS
Capital: Minsk
Area: 207,600 sq km (80,134 sq miles)
Population: 9,800,000
Languages: Belarussian, Russian

ESTONIA
Capital: Tallinn
Area: 45,100 sq km (17,413 sq miles)
Population: 1,300,000
Language: Estonian

GEORGIA
Capital: T'bilisi
Area: 69,700 sq km (26,900 sq miles)
Population: 4,500,000
Language: Georgian

KAZAKHSTAN
Capital: Astana
Area: 2,717,300 sq km (1,049,155 sq miles)
Population: 14,800,000
Languages: Kazakh, Russian

KYRGYZSTAN
Capital: Bishkek
Area: 198,500 sq km (76,640 sq miles)
Population: 5,300,000
Languages: Kyrgyz, Russian

LATVIA
Capital: Riga
Area: 63,700 sq km (24,595 sq miles)
Population: 2,300,000
Languages: Latvian, Russian

LITHUANIA
Capital: Vilnius
Area: 65,200 sq km (25,170 sq miles)
Population: 3,400,000
Language: Lithuanian

MOLDOVA
Capital: Chisinau
Area: 33,700 sq km (13,000 sq miles)
Population: 4,200,000
Languages: Romanian, Moldovan

RUSSIAN FEDERATION
Capital: Moscow
Area: 17,075,000 sq km (6,592,637 sq miles)
Population: 143,000,000
Language: Russian

TAJIKISTAN
Capital: Dushanbe
Area: 143,100 sq km (55,240 sq miles)
Population: 6,500,000
Languages: Tajik, Russian

TURKMENISTAN
Capital: Ashgabat
Area: 488,100 sq km (188,455 sq miles)
Population: 4,800,000
Languages: Turkmen, Russian

UKRAINE
Capital: Kiev
Area: 603,700 sq km (231,990 sq miles)
Population: 46,500,000
Languages: Ukrainian, Russian

UZBEKISTAN
Capital: Tashkent
Area: 447,400 sq km (172,741 sq miles)
Population: 26,600,000
Languages: Uzbek, Russian

UNITED STATES AND CANADA

The countries that form North America are two of the largest and richest in the world; Canada is second only to the Russian Federation in land area, yet it has only about one tenth the population of the United States, its smaller neighbour. Canada has ten provinces and three territories, while the United States is made up of 50 states plus the District of Columbia (D.C.) where Washington, the capital, is located.

The original inhabitants of North America were once called 'Indians'; Canadian tribes are now more correctly known as 'First Nation' people, and those of the U.S. as 'Native Americans'. Similarly, the term 'Eskimo', previously used for natives of the far north, has been replaced by 'Inuit'. Today, the population of both countries is a mix of racial backgrounds: European, African, Asian, and Hispanic (Spanish speaking) from Central and South America.

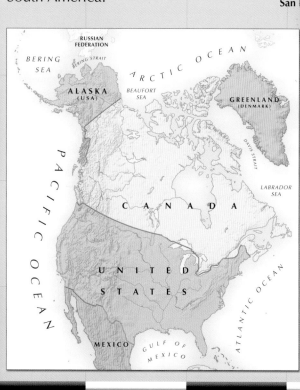

RUSSIAN FEDERATION
BERING SEA
BERING STRAIT
ARCTIC OCEAN
ALASKA (USA)
BEAUFORT SEA
GREENLAND (DENMARK)
PACIFIC OCEAN
DAVIS STRAIT
CANADA
LABRADOR SEA
UNITED STATES
ATLANTIC OCEAN
MEXICO
GULF OF MEXICO

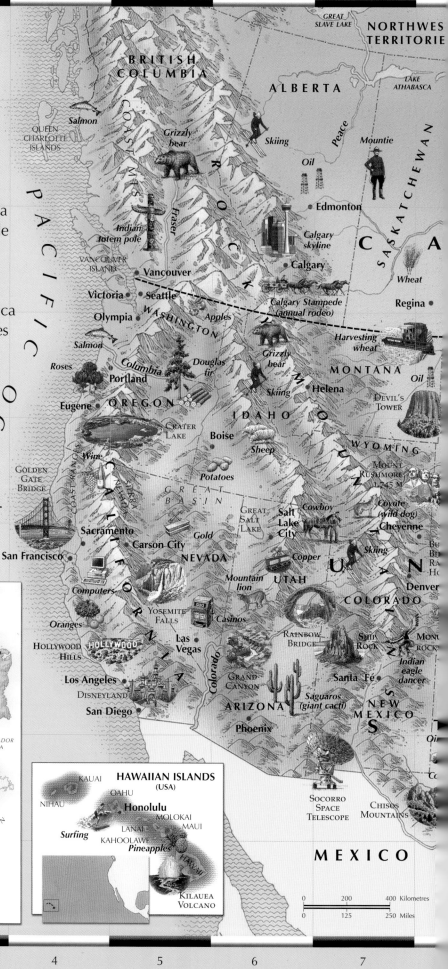

GREAT SLAVE LAKE
NORTHWEST TERRITORIE
BRITISH COLUMBIA
ALBERTA
LAKE ATHABASCA
Salmon
Grizzly bear
Skiing
Peace
Mountie
QUEEN CHARLOTTE ISLANDS
COAST MTS
Oil
SASKATCHEWAN
ROCKY
Fraser
Edmonton
Indian Totem pole
Calgary skyline
CA
VANCOUVER ISLAND
Vancouver
Calgary
Victoria Seattle
Wheat
Olympia
WASHINGTON
Apples
Calgary Stampede (annual rodeo)
Regina
PACIFIC
Salmon
Harvesting wheat
Roses
Columbia
Douglas fir
Grizzly bear
MONTANA
Oil
Portland
OREGON
Skiing
Helena
DEVIL'S TOWER
Eugene
CRATER LAKE
Boise
IDAHO
WYOMING
OCEAN
Wine
Sheep
MOUNT RUSHMORE 1,745 M
Potatoes
GREAT BASIN
Coyote (wild dog)
GOLDEN GATE BRIDGE
Cowboy
GREAT SALT LAKE
Salt Lake City
Cheyenne
COAST RANGES
SIERRA NEVADA
Sacramento
Gold
Copper
Skiing
Carson City
NEVADA
UT
Denver
San Francisco
Mountain lion
UTAH
COLORADO
Computers
CALIFORNIA
YOSEMITE FALLS
Casinos
RAINBOW BRIDGE
SHIP ROCK
MON ROCK
Oranges
Las Vegas
Indian eagle dancer
HOLLYWOOD HILLS
HOLLYWOOD
Colorado
GRAND CANYON
Santa Fé
NEW MEXICO
Los Angeles
DISNEYLAND
Saguaros (giant cacti)
San Diego
ARIZONA
Phoenix
SOCORRO SPACE TELESCOPE
CHISOS MOUNTAINS
MEXICO

HAWAIIAN ISLANDS (USA)
KAUAI
OAHU
NIHAU
Honolulu
MOLOKAI
MAUI
Surfing
LANAI
KAHOOLAWE
Pineapples
HAWAII
KILAUEA VOLCANO

0   200   400 Kilometres
0   125   250 Miles

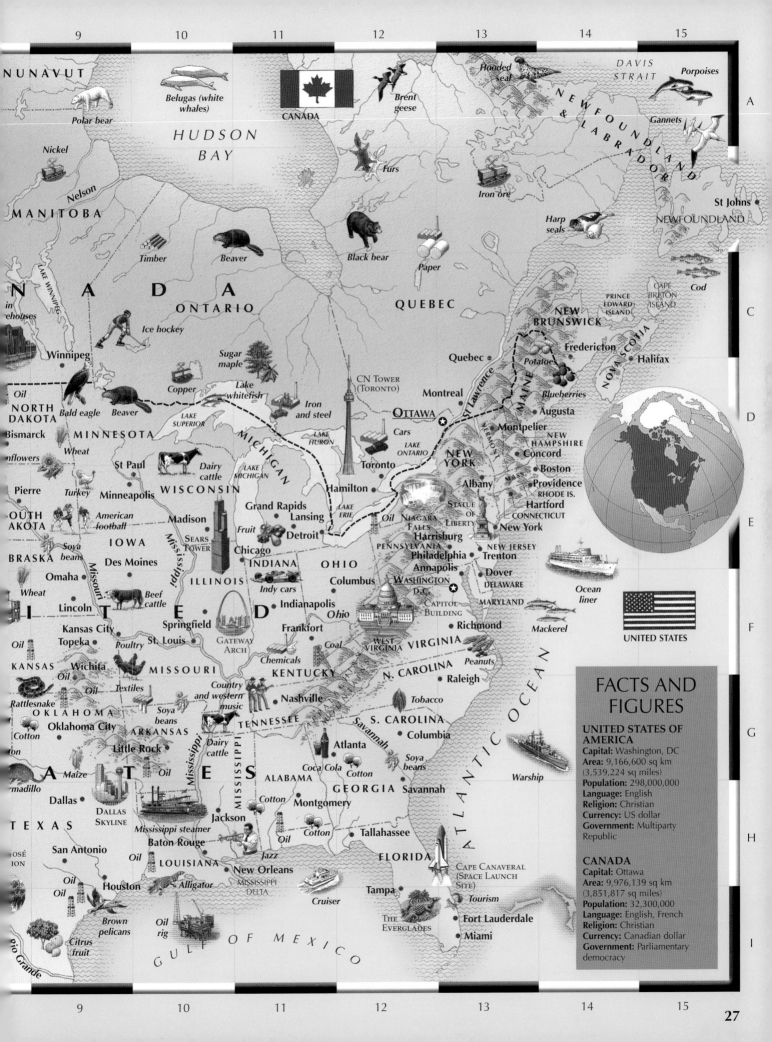

Map of North America (United States and Canada) with grid coordinates 9–15 across the top and bottom, and A–I down the right side.

Canada (northern region)

NUNAVUT

Polar bear · Nickel · Nelson

Belugas (white whales) · HUDSON BAY · Brent geese

CANADA (flag)

Hooded seal · Porpoises · DAVIS STRAIT

Gannets · NEWFOUNDLAND & LABRADOR · St Johns

MANITOBA · Furs · Iron ore · Harp seals · NEWFOUNDLAND

Timber · Beaver · Black bear · Paper · Cod

CAPE BRETON ISLAND · PRINCE EDWARD ISLAND

in arehouses · Lake Winnipeg · Ice hockey · ONTARIO · QUEBEC · NEW BRUNSWICK · Fredericton · Halifax · NOVA SCOTIA

Winnipeg · Sugar maple · Quebec · Potatoes · Blueberries

Oil · Copper · Lake whitefish · CN TOWER (TORONTO) · Montreal · Augusta · MAINE

NORTH DAKOTA · Bald eagle · Beaver · LAKE SUPERIOR · Iron and steel · St Lawrence · Montpelier · NEW HAMPSHIRE

Bismarck · MINNESOTA · LAKE MICHIGAN · LAKE HURON · Cars · VERMONT · Concord

Wheat · St Paul · Dairy cattle · Toronto · LAKE ONTARIO · NEW YORK · Albany · Boston

nflowers · Pierre · Turkey · Minneapolis · WISCONSIN · Grand Rapids · Hamilton · LAKE ERIE · Providence · RHODE IS.

SOUTH DAKOTA · American football · Madison · Lansing · Oil · NIAGARA FALLS · Harrisburg · Hartford · CONNECTICUT

IOWA · SEARS TOWER · Fruit · Detroit · STATUE OF LIBERTY · New York

BRASKA · Soya beans · Des Moines · Chicago · INDIANA · OHIO · PENNSYLVANIA · Philadelphia · Trenton · NEW JERSEY

Omaha · ILLINOIS · Indy cars · Columbus · Annapolis · Dover · DELAWARE

Wheat · Lincoln · Beef cattle · Springfield · Indianapolis · Ohio · WASHINGTON D.C. · MARYLAND · Ocean liner

UNITED STATES (flag)

Oil · Topeka · Kansas City · Poultry · GATEWAY ARCH · Frankfort · CAPITOL BUILDING · Richmond · Mackerel

KANSAS · Wichita · St. Louis · Chemicals · Coal · WEST VIRGINIA · VIRGINIA

Oil · Oil · Textiles · MISSOURI · KENTUCKY · Peanuts · Raleigh

Rattlesnake · Country and western music · Nashville · N. CAROLINA

OKLAHOMA · Soya beans · TENNESSEE · Tobacco

Cotton · Oklahoma City · ARKANSAS · Dairy cattle · Savannah · S. CAROLINA · Columbia

bon · Little Rock · Coca Cola · Atlanta · Soya beans

Maize · Oil · Cotton · ALABAMA · Cotton · GEORGIA · Savannah

Dallas · DALLAS SKYLINE · Jackson · MISSISSIPPI · Montgomery · Warship

osé ion · San Antonio · Mississippi steamer · Cotton · Oil · Cotton · Tallahassee

TEXAS · Baton Rouge · Jazz · FLORIDA · Cape Canaveral (Space Launch Site)

Oil · LOUISIANA · New Orleans · Oil · Tampa · ATLANTIC OCEAN

Oil · Houston · Alligator · MISSISSIPPI DELTA · Cruiser · Tourism

Oil · Oil rig · Brown pelicans · THE EVERGLADES · Fort Lauderdale · Miami

Rio Grande · Citrus fruit · GULF OF MEXICO

FACTS AND FIGURES

UNITED STATES OF AMERICA
Capital: Washington, DC
Area: 9,166,600 sq km (3,539,224 sq miles)
Population: 298,000,000
Language: English
Religion: Christian
Currency: US dollar
Government: Multiparty Republic

CANADA
Capital: Ottawa
Area: 9,976,139 sq km (3,851,817 sq miles)
Population: 32,300,000
Language: English, French
Religion: Christian
Currency: Canadian dollar
Government: Parliamentary democracy

MEXICO AND CENTRAL AMERICA

CENTRAL AMERICA IS a land bridge joining the continents of North and South America. At its narrowest point, in Panama, a canal 82 km (51 miles) long links the Atlantic and Pacific oceans. There are seven countries in Central America. To the north lies Mexico and to the east lie the islands of the Caribbean, which are often called the West Indies. In the Caribbean, local poverty and tourist luxury exist side by side.

During the 16th century, the islands were settled by Europeans, who shipped black slaves from Africa to work on the farms. Today the population is a mixture of many peoples. The main languages are English, Spanish, and dialects called patois: mixtures of African languages with French or English.

There are great contrasts in the area's climate and vegetation, from the Mexican desert in the north to the southern rainforests and the coral islands in the east. Sometimes tropical storms called hurricanes rage through the Caribbean, their high winds and huge waves causing devastating damage.

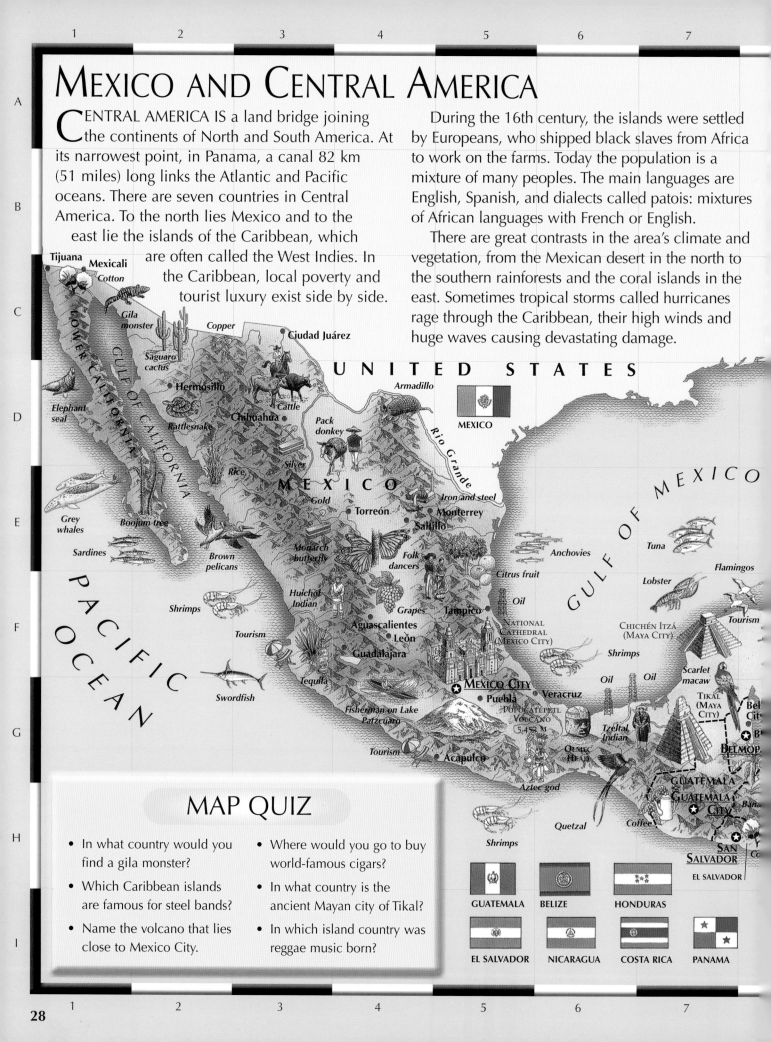

Tijuana
Mexicali
Cotton
Gila monster
Copper
Ciudad Juárez
Saguaro cactus
Hermosillo
Armadillo
Elephant seal
Cattle
Chihuahua
Pack donkey
Rattlesnake
Rio Grande
UNITED STATES
MEXICO
GULF OF CALIFORNIA
LOWER CALIFORNIA
Rice
Silver
MEXICO
Grey whales
Boojum tree
Gold
Torreón
Monterrey
Saltillo
GULF OF MEXICO
Sardines
Brown pelicans
Monarch butterfly
Folk dancers
Anchovies
Tuna
Flamingos
Citrus fruit
Lobster
Shrimps
Huichol Indian
Oil
Tourism
Grapes
Tampico
Shrimps
CHICHÉN ITZÁ (MAYA CITY)
Aguascalientes
León
NATIONAL CATHEDRAL (MEXICO CITY)
Scarlet macaw
Guadalajara
Tequila
Swordfish
MEXICO CITY
Puebla
Veracruz
Oil
Oil
TIKAL (MAYA CITY)
Bel Cit
Fisherman on Lake Pátzcuaro
POPOCATÉPETL VOLCANO 5,452 M
B
Tzéltal Indian
BELMO
Tourism
Acapulco
OLMEC HEAD
GUATEMALA
Aztec god
GUATEMALA CITY
Bañ
Quetzal
Coffee
Shrimps
SAN SALVADOR
Co
EL SALVADOR

MAP QUIZ

- In what country would you find a gila monster?
- Which Caribbean islands are famous for steel bands?
- Name the volcano that lies close to Mexico City.
- Where would you go to buy world-famous cigars?
- In what country is the ancient Mayan city of Tikal?
- In which island country was reggae music born?

GUATEMALA   BELIZE   HONDURAS

EL SALVADOR   NICARAGUA   COSTA RICA   PANAMA

FACTS AND FIGURES

Jamaica ("island of springs") is a popular tourist resort.

ANTIGUA & BARBUDA
Capital: St John's
ARUBA
Capital: Oranjestad
BAHAMAS
Capital: Nassau
BARBADOS
Capital: Bridgetown
BELIZE
Capital: Belmopan
COSTA RICA
Capital: San José

CUBA
Capital: Havana
DOMINICA
Capital: Roseau
DOMINICAN REPUBLIC
Capital: Santo Domingo
EL SALVADOR
Capital: San Salvador
GRENADA
Capital: St George's
GUADELOUPE
Capital: Basse Terre
GUATEMALA
Capital: Guatemala City
HAITI
Capital: Port-au-Prince
HONDURAS
Capital: Tegucigalpa
JAMAICA
Capital: Kingston

MARTINIQUE
Capital: Fort-de-France
MEXICO
Capital: Mexico City
NETHERLANDS ANTILLES
Capital: Willemstad
NICARAGUA
Capital: Managua
PANAMA
Capital: Panama City
PUERTO RICO
Capital: San Juan
ST KITTS & NEVIS
Capital: Basseterre
ST LUCIA
Capital: Castries
ST VINCENT & THE GRENADINES
Capital: Kingstown
TRINIDAD & TOBAGO
Capital: Port-of-Spain

DOMINICA

ST LUCIA

ST KITTS & NEVIS

ANTIGUA & BARBUDA — BAHAMAS — ST VINCENT & THE GRENADINES — BARBADOS — GRENADA — TRINIDAD & TOBAGO

CUBA — JAMAICA — HAITI — DOMINICAN REPUBLIC

ATLANTIC OCEAN

UNITED STATES

Tourism

BAHAMAS
Nassau
Cruise liner
Scuba diver

STRAITS OF FLORIDA

Sugar cane
Coral reefs
HAVANA
CUBA
Pineapples
Cigars
Scuba diver
CAYMAN ISLANDS (UK)
JAMAICA
Kingston
Reggae music
Rum
Green turtle
Grapefruit

TURKS & CAICOS ISLANDS (UK)
Cocoa
Coffee
HAITI
DOMINICAN REPUBLIC
Port-au-Prince
Santo Domingo
Sharks

Coral reefs
Tourism
VIRGIN ISLANDS (USA/UK)
San Juan
PUERTO RICO (US)
Sailing

Frigate bird
ANGUILLA (UK)
ST KITTS & NEVIS
MONTSERRAT (UK)
ANTIGUA & BARBUDA
GUADELOUPE (Fr)
Coconuts
DOMINICA
MARTINIQUE (Fr)
ST LUCIA
BARBADOS
ST VINCENT & THE GRENADINES

Nutmeg and mace
GRENADA
Steel bands
TRINIDAD & TOBAGO

CARIBBEAN SEA

HONDURAS
Cattle
TEGUCIGALPA
Coffee
Bananas
NICARAGUA
MANAGUA
Coffee
SAN JOSÉ
COSTA RICA
PANAMA
PANAMA CANAL
PANAMA CITY
Spider monkey
Toucan

ARUBA (Neth)
NETHERLANDS ANTILLES (Neth)
COLOMBIA
VENEZUELA

0 200 400 600 800 Kilometres
0 100 200 300 400 500 Miles

SOUTH AMERICA

THE CONTINENT OF South America is dominated by the snow-capped Andes mountains and the wide Amazon river, which flows through the vast rainforests of the north. South of the Amazon are the grassy plains of the Pampas and vast expanses of barren, windswept desert. South America's wealth comes from agriculture, tourism and the export of beef. Natural resources such as coal, copper, gold, iron ore, lead, natural gas, oil and tin also contribute. During the 16th century, the land was settled by Europeans, who conquered many of the native peoples. Among these were the Incas, whose civilization flourished in the Peruvian Andes until it was destroyed in 1532-33 by Spanish conquistadors.

URUGUAY

SURINAM

VENEZUELA

PERU

GUYANA

COLOMBIA

BRAZIL

BOLIVIA

ECUADOR

PARAGUAY

ARGENTINA

CHILE

ATLANTIC OCEAN

PACIFIC

PANAMA

A N D E S M

BRAZIL

GUYANA

VENEZUELA

COLOMBIA

ECUADOR

PERU

SURINAM

FRENCH GUIANA (France)

Natal

Recife

CHURCH OF OUR LADY OF CARMO

Salvador

Cocoa pods

Fortaleza

Bananas

Teresina

Brazil nuts

Brasília

BRASÍLIA CATHEDRAL DOME

São Francisco

Tocantins

Kayapo Indian

Araguaia

Suya Indian

Jangada fishing raft

Lobster

Green turtle

Water buffalo

Belém

MARAJÓ ISLAND

Mango tree

Gold

Gold and blue macaw

Xingu

Umbrella bird

CAYENNE

Ariane Rocket Launch Site

Wayana Indian

Amazon

Anaconda

Caiman

GEORGETOWN

PARAMARIBO

MANAUS OPERA HOUSE

Manaus

Humming bird

Porto Velho

Negro

Capybara (world's largest rodent)

Rainforest

Rubber trees

Two-toed sloth

Purus

Madeira

Scarlet ibis

CARACAS

Valencia

Ciudad Bolívar

ANGEL FALLS

Diamonds

Red howler monkey

Indian hunter

MACHU PICCHU

Barquisimeto

Harpy eagle

Orinoco

Jaguar

Iquitos

Toco toucan

Llama

Barranquilla

Cartagena

BOGOTÁ

BOGOTÁ CATHEDRAL

Pre-Columbian stone idol

Peruvian cock-of-the-rock

Cavies (guinea pigs)

Indian flute players

Medellín

Manizales

Cali

Emeralds

COTOPAXI 5,897 M

QUITO

Bananas

Coffee

Piura

HUASCARAN 6,768 M

LIMA

Chiclayo

Trujillo

ATLANTIC OCEAN

FALKLAND ISLANDS (UK)

Sheep
STANLEY
Albatross
Rock hopper penguins

200 Kilometres / 150 Miles
100 / 50
0 / 0

Hake

ATLANTIC OCEAN

Dusky dolphins

800 Kilometres / 500 Miles
600 / 375
400 / 250
200 / 125
0 / 0

MAP QUIZ

- In what type of ranching would a gaucho be employed?
- What is the name of the ancient Inca city in Peru?
- Which capital city features a dramatic domed cathedral?
- West of the Andes mountains, in northern Chile, is a huge desert. What is it called?
- In which country is the Ariane Rocket Launch Site?
- What is a carreta?
- Lake Titicaca is the highest navigable lake in the world. Where is it?
- Sugar Loaf Mountain stands at the entrance to a famous South American harbour city. Which one is it?

Map labels

Shrimps
CORCOVADO STATUE OF CHRIST (RIO DE JANEIRO)
SUGAR LOAF MT 395 M
Belo Horizonte
Rio de Janeiro
Humming bird
São Paulo
Campinas
Carnival
Football
Cars
Coffee
Oranges
Curitiba
MATO GROSSO
Campo Grande
Jabiru stork
Cotton
PORTO ALEGRE CATHEDRAL
Porto Alegre
Tobacco
Puva raimondii (world's Tallest herb)
Santa Cruz
Cochabamba
BOLIVIA
SUCRE
Concepción
ASUNCIÓN
PARAGUAY
GRAN CHACO
Paraná
Paraguay
Corrientes
Resistencia
Maté (type of tea)
Salado
Santa Fe
Paraná
Rosario
URUGUAY
Uruguay
Tourism
MONTEVIDEO
BUENOS AIRES
COLON OPERA HOUSE
La Plata
RIVER PLATE
Mar del Plata
Tango dancers
Tourism
Bolivian Indians
Arica
Iquique
Antofagasta
ATACAMA DESERT
LICANCABUR VOLCANO 5,921 M
Carreta (ox-drawn cart)
San Miguel de Tucumán
Santiago del Estero
Córdoba
San Juan
Wine
OLOS DEL SALADO 6,880 M
Cherries
Mt ACONCAGUA 6,959 M
Viña del Mar
Valparaíso
Mackerel
Rancagua
SANTIAGO
Concepción
CHILE
Huaso (Chilean cowboy)
Trout
Salmon
Mendoza
ARGENTINA
PAMPAS
Gaucho (cattleherder)
Colorado
Negro
Atuel
Maned wolf
Darwin's rhea
ANDES MTS
Bahía Blanca
Right whale
Chubut
Chico
Oil
Comodoro Rivadavia
Sealions
Sheep
Timber
Salmon
Fur seals
MORENO GLACIER
Punta Arenas
STRAIT OF MAGELLAN
TIERRA DEL FUEGO
Ushuaia
CAPE HORN
Río Gallegos
Oil
PATAGONIA

GALAPAGOS ISLANDS (ECUADOR)

Galapagos giant tortoise
Marine iguana
ISABELA ISLAND

200 Kilometres / 150 Miles
100 / 75
0 / 0

FACTS AND FIGURES

Highest mountains:
Mt Aconcagua (Argentina), 6,959 m (22,831 ft); Ojos del Salado (Argentina-Chile), 6,880 m (22,572 ft); Huascarán (Peru), 6,768 m (22,205 ft); Illimani (Bolivia), 6,402 m (21,004 ft).

Longest rivers:
Amazon, 6,437 km (4,000 miles); Paraná, 4,500 km (2,796 miles); Madeira, 3,199 km (1,988 miles); São Francisco, 3,199 km (1,988 miles); Purús, 2,993 km (1,860 miles).

Largest lake:
Lake Titicaca (Peru-Bolivia), 8,340 sq km (3,220 sq miles).

World's highest waterfall:
Angel Falls (Venezuela), 979 m (3,212 ft).

Largest cities:
São Paulo (Brazil), 20,218,868; Buenos Aires (Argentina), 14,197,085; Rio de Janeiro (Brazil), 11,975,998; Lima (Peru), 7,804,611; Santiago (Chile), 5,099,129.

World's leading coffee grower:
Brazil grows around 4,000,000 tonnes (3,936,826 tons) of coffee each year.

31

THE MIDDLE EAST

T HE MIDDLE EAST (also known as southwest Asia) lies at the join of three continents – Asia, Africa, and Europe – and takes in many different landscapes. There is a wide variety too, in cultures and religions, and these differences have resulted in longstanding political instability in the region.

The countries surrounding the Mediterranean are wetter than the others, and crops such as citrus fruits, olives and wheat are grown there. To the south stretch the huge deserts of Saudi Arabia. In the mid 20th century, the world's largest deposits of oil were discovered in the countries around the Gulf, and the oil-fields in the region now supply the world.

Some of the world's first settled farming communities grew up in the Fertile Crescent, which stretches from the Mediterranean to the area between the Tigris and Euphrates rivers. Of great historical interest, too, is the city of Jerusalem, which is a holy place for Christians, Muslims and Jews, visited by millions of people each year.

SYRIA

LEBANON

ISRAEL

JORDAN

CYPRUS

SAUDI ARABIA

MAP QUIZ

- An old Syrian city gives its name to a luxurious textile weave. What is it?

- The ancient city of Baghdad lies on what river?

- Which sea is known for its caviar-producing sturgeon?

- What is a traditional Arab sailing boat called?

- From which tree does the biblical perfume called Frankincense come?

- A country in this region has the same name as its capital city. Which one is it?

- What mountain range borders the Gulf in Iran?

- On which sea does the city of Jedda lie?

- Can you find two textile fibres that are produced in the Middle East?

- Muslim women cover their faces in public. What is the name of the veil they wear?

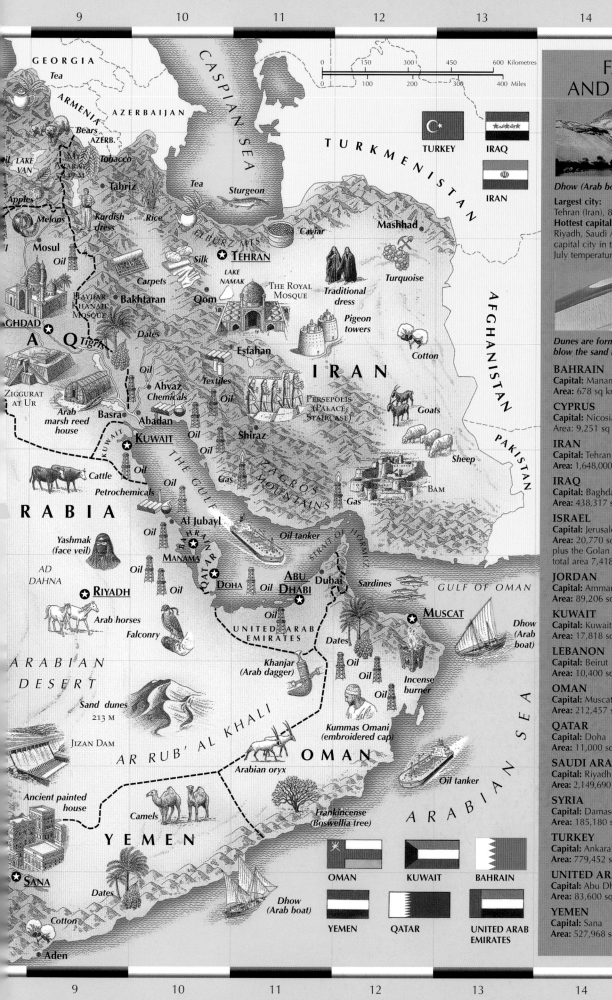

GEORGIA
Tea
ARMENIA
Bears
AZERB.
AZERBAIJAN
Tobacco
IL LAKE VAN
MT ARARAT
Apples
Melons
Mosul
Oil
Kurdish dress
Tabriz
Rice
Tea
CASPIAN SEA
Sturgeon
Caviar
Mashhad
TURKMENISTAN
ELBURZ MTS
Silk
TEHRAN
LAKE NAMAK
Carpets
Bakhtaran
Qom
THE ROYAL MOSQUE
Traditional dress
Turquoise
Pigeon towers
AFGHANISTAN
GHDAD
HAYDAR KHANAH MOSQUE
Dates
Esfahan
Cotton
A Q
Tigris
IRAN
PAKISTAN
Oil
Ahvaz
Chemicals
Textiles
Oil
PERSEPOLIS (PALACE STAIRCASE)
Goats
ZIGGURAT AT UR
Arab marsh reed house
Basra
Abadan
KUWAIT
Oil
Shiraz
ZAGROS MOUNTAINS
Sheep
Bam
KUWAIT
Oil
Oil
RABIA
Cattle
Oil
Petrochemicals
Oil
Gas
Gas
Yashmak (face veil)
Al Jubayl
Oil tanker
STRAIT OF HORMUZ
AD DAHNA
Oil
MANAMA
Oil
GULF OF OMAN
RIYADH
DOHA
Oil
ABU DHABI
Dubai
Sardines
Oil
MUSCAT
Dhow (Arab boat)
Arab horses
Falconry
Oil
UNITED ARAB EMIRATES
Dates
ARABIAN DESERT
Khanjar (Arab dagger)
Oil
Oil
Incense burner
Sand dunes 213 M
ARABIAN SEA
AR RUB' AL KHALI
Kummas Omani (embroidered cap)
OMAN
Jizan Dam
Arabian oryx
Oil tanker
Ancient painted house
Camels
Frankincense (Boswellia tree)
YEMEN
SANA
Dates
Dhow (Arab boat)
Cotton
Aden

TURKEY
IRAQ
IRAN

OMAN KUWAIT BAHRAIN
YEMEN QATAR UNITED ARAB EMIRATES

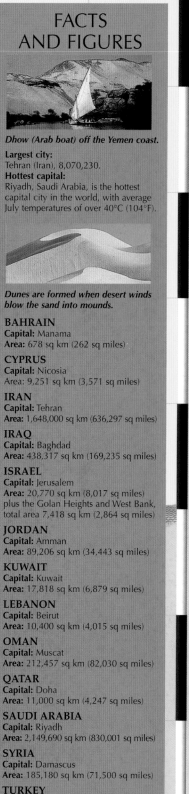

FACTS AND FIGURES

Dhow (Arab boat) off the Yemen coast.

Largest city:
Tehran (Iran), 8,070,230.
Hottest capital:
Riyadh, Saudi Arabia, is the hottest capital city in the world, with average July temperatures of over 40°C (104°F).

Dunes are formed when desert winds blow the sand into mounds.

BAHRAIN
Capital: Manama
Area: 678 sq km (262 sq miles)

CYPRUS
Capital: Nicosia
Area: 9,251 sq km (3,571 sq miles)

IRAN
Capital: Tehran
Area: 1,648,000 sq km (636,297 sq miles)

IRAQ
Capital: Baghdad
Area: 438,317 sq km (169,235 sq miles)

ISRAEL
Capital: Jerusalem
Area: 20,770 sq km (8,017 sq miles) plus the Golan Heights and West Bank, total area 7,418 sq km (2,864 sq miles)

JORDAN
Capital: Amman
Area: 89,206 sq km (34,443 sq miles)

KUWAIT
Capital: Kuwait
Area: 17,818 sq km (6,879 sq miles)

LEBANON
Capital: Beirut
Area: 10,400 sq km (4,015 sq miles)

OMAN
Capital: Muscat
Area: 212,457 sq km (82,030 sq miles)

QATAR
Capital: Doha
Area: 11,000 sq km (4,247 sq miles)

SAUDI ARABIA
Capital: Riyadh
Area: 2,149,690 sq km (830,001 sq miles)

SYRIA
Capital: Damascus
Area: 185,180 sq km (71,500 sq miles)

TURKEY
Capital: Ankara
Area: 779,452 sq km (300,948 sq miles)

UNITED ARAB EMIRATES
Capital: Abu Dhabi
Area: 83,600 sq km (32,278 sq miles)

YEMEN
Capital: Sana
Area: 527,968 sq km (203,850 sq miles)

Southern Asia

THE LARGEST COUNTRY in Southern Asia is India, and the region is often called the "Indian subcontinent". Over one billion people live there – about 22 per cent of the world's population. Most people live in the fertile river and coastal plains. Nearly three-quarters are farmers, who depend heavily on seasonal rains. The most important crop is rice.

India was united in the 16th and 17th centuries under Mogul rule. In the 18th century, it became part of the British Empire, but gained independence in 1947, when it was divided into two: Hindu India and Muslim Pakistan. In 1971, east Pakistan became a separate country, Bangladesh.

Today, Pakistan and India are industrial nations. Pakistan's industries include food processing, textiles and chemicals. India produces oil, coal, manganese, iron ore, and copper, and has iron and steel, car manufacturing, and computer industries.

MAP QUIZ

- Hindu people believe the Ganges River is holy. In which mountain range is its source?

- Through what countries does the region's longest river, the Indus, flow?

- Where could you see 'giraffe-necked' women with metal rings around their throat?

- In which city is the huge Victoria Railway Terminus?

- Name the traditional Indian loincloth woven from undyed, homespun cotton.

- Can you locate the highest mountain in Southern Asia?

- What island is famous for its thriving trade in tea?

- Which stringed instrument, sometimes used in western music, is associated with India?

- What two countries are linked by the Kyber Pass?

- Where would you go to find both ruby and jade mines?

- In Burma (Myanmar), which animal is used to haul heavy teak logs?

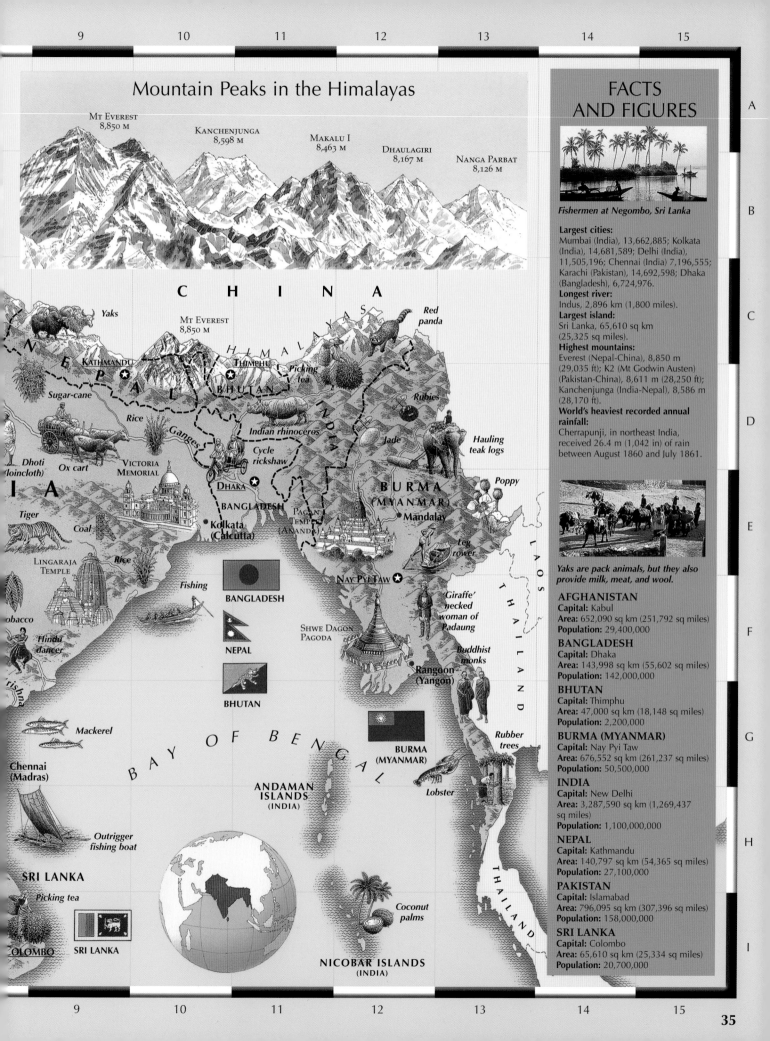

Mountain Peaks in the Himalayas

Mt Everest
8,850 M

Kanchenjunga
8,598 M

Makalu I
8,463 M

Dhaulagiri
8,167 M

Nanga Parbat
8,126 M

FACTS AND FIGURES

Fishermen at Negombo, Sri Lanka

Largest cities:
Mumbai (India), 13,662,885; Kolkata (India), 14,681,589; Delhi (India), 11,505,196; Chennai (India) 7,196,555; Karachi (Pakistan), 14,692,598; Dhaka (Bangladesh), 6,724,976.
Longest river:
Indus, 2,896 km (1,800 miles).
Largest island:
Sri Lanka, 65,610 sq km (25,325 sq miles).
Highest mountains:
Everest (Nepal-China), 8,850 m (29,035 ft); K2 (Mt Godwin Austen) (Pakistan-China), 8,611 m (28,250 ft); Kanchenjunga (India-Nepal), 8,586 m (28,170 ft).
World's heaviest recorded annual rainfall:
Cherrapunji, in northeast India, received 26.4 m (1,042 in) of rain between August 1860 and July 1861.

Yaks are pack animals, but they also provide milk, meat, and wool.

AFGHANISTAN
Capital: Kabul
Area: 652,090 sq km (251,792 sq miles)
Population: 29,400,000

BANGLADESH
Capital: Dhaka
Area: 143,998 sq km (55,602 sq miles)
Population: 142,000,000

BHUTAN
Capital: Thimphu
Area: 47,000 sq km (18,148 sq miles)
Population: 2,200,000

BURMA (MYANMAR)
Capital: Nay Pyi Taw
Area: 676,552 sq km (261,237 sq miles)
Population: 50,500,000

INDIA
Capital: New Delhi
Area: 3,287,590 sq km (1,269,437 sq miles)
Population: 1,100,000,000

NEPAL
Capital: Kathmandu
Area: 140,797 sq km (54,365 sq miles)
Population: 27,100,000

PAKISTAN
Capital: Islamabad
Area: 796,095 sq km (307,396 sq miles)
Population: 158,000,000

SRI LANKA
Capital: Colombo
Area: 65,610 sq km (25,334 sq miles)
Population: 20,700,000

Map labels

CHINA

NEPAL

Yaks

Mt Everest
8,850 M

KATHMANDU

Sugar-cane

Rice

Ox cart

Ganges

Dhoti (loincloth)

VICTORIA MEMORIAL

Tiger

Coal

Rice

LINGARAJA TEMPLE

Tobacco

Hindu dancer

Krishna

Mackerel

Chennai (Madras)

Outrigger fishing boat

SRI LANKA

Picking tea

COLOMBO

Fishing

BANGLADESH

NEPAL

BHUTAN

THIMPHU

Picking tea

BHUTAN

Indian rhinoceros

Cycle rickshaw

DHAKA

BANGLADESH

Kolkata (Calcutta)

HIMALAYAS

INDIA

Red panda

Rubies

Jade

Hauling teak logs

Poppy

BURMA (MYANMAR)

Mandalay

Pagan Temple (Ananda)

NAY PYI TAW

Leg rower

'Giraffe' necked woman of Padaung

Buddhist monks

Rangoon (Yangon)

SHWE DAGON PAGODA

BURMA (MYANMAR)

LAOS

THAILAND

Rubber trees

Lobster

Coconut palms

BAY OF BENGAL

ANDAMAN ISLANDS (INDIA)

NICOBAR ISLANDS (INDIA)

THAILAND

JAPAN

LYING EAST OF THE MAIN PART of Asia, Japan is made up of four major islands – Hokkaido, Honshu, Shikoku, and Kyushu – and thousands of smaller ones. In this area, where two plates of the Earth's crust meet, earthquakes are common.

Nearly three-quarters of the country is mountainous and wooded, but the areas that are suitable for agriculture are cultivated very efficiently. The main crop is rice. Because so little of the land can be farmed, the Japanese eat a lot of fish, and they catch more fish than any other nation. Most of Japan's 126 million people live on a small area of flat, largely coastal, land, mainly around the great south-coast cities of Honshu island, such as Nagoya, Tokyo and Osaka.

In the last 40 years Japan has become one of the world's most important industrial nations. This is all the more remarkable because the oil and most of the raw materials that are needed in manufacturing have to be imported. Japanese cars, electrical goods, ships, cameras, and many other products are exported all over the world.

MAP QUIZ

- Mount Fuji, Japan's highest mountain, is located on which of the four main islands?

- For more than 1,000 years, the city of Kyoto was the capital of Japan. Where is Kyoto?

- Which style of formal wrestling originated in Japan?

- An important religious shrine is shown on Honshu island. What faith does it represent?

- What kind of food is tofu?

- Can you find the location of an annual snow festival?

- Name a type of theatre that is popular in Japan.

- Which gem is found in the seas around Japan?

- What is the name of the ancient fortified castle on the Japanese island of Shikoku?

- Miniature trees are highly prized in Japanese culture. What are they called?

KURIL ISLANDS (RUSS. FED.)

PACIFIC OCEAN

HOKKAIDO

JAPAN

Nemuro
Japanese crane
Trout
Ceremonial Ainu dress
Kushiro
Pollock
Steller's sea eagle
Teshio
Fishing boats
Saury
Timber
Paper
Brown bear
Coal
Potatoes
Muroran
Sapporo
Snow festival
MT YOTEI 1,893 M
Fish owl
Cod
Hakodate
Fukushima
TAPPI-ZAKI
Halibut
Aomori
Apples
Sake
Akita
Morioka
Bonsai (miniature trees)
Mackerel
Oysters
Judo
Japanese arts
Sendai
Crab
Coal
Rice planting
Fukushima
Automatic rice planter
Fish flags (carp streamers)
Sardines
Anchovies

FACTS AND FIGURES

Highest mountain:
Mt Fuji, 3,776 m (12,388 ft).

Main ports:
Tokyo, Yokohama, Osaka, Kobe.

Wettest area:
All of Japan has high rainfall, but the wettest place is the southernmost island of Kyushu, where average rainfall reaches over 2,200 mm (86.6 in) per year.

Coldest area:
Hokkaido has average winter temperatures of -10°C (14°F).

Food:
Only 15 per cent of the land, mostly on the coastal plains, can be farmed. But despite this, Japan is 70 per cent self-sufficient in food.

World's largest fishing fleet:
Japan catches around 14 per cent of the total world catch – more than any other country. Each Japanese person eats an average of 30 kg (65 lbs) of fish a year.

World's longest railway tunnel:
The Seikan Rail Tunnel in Japan runs for 53.85 km (33.46 miles) between the headland of Tappi-Zaki on Honshu island and the small town of Fukushima on Hokkaido.

World's longest suspension bridge:
The Akashi-Kaikyo Bridge links Awaji Island to Honshu. Also known as the Pearl Bridge it has a main span (distance between the towers) of 1,991 m (6,532 ft).

World's top oil importer:
Japan. The Seawise Giant, a Japanese tanker built in 1981, is the largest tanker in the world. It is almost 500 m (547 yards) long and can carry 565,000 tonnes of crude oil.

Largest cities:
Tokyo, 8,483,050; Yokohama, 3,579,133; Osaka, 2,628,776; Nagoya, 2,215,031; Sapporo, 1,880,875; Kobe, 1,525,389; Kyoto, 1,474,764; Fukuoka, 1,400,621.

Four largest islands:
Honshu, Hokkaido, Kyushu, Shikoku.

A Japanese garden in Hiroshima.

Tokyo, Japan's bustling capital.

JAPAN
Capital: Tokyo
Area: 377,801 sq km (145,835 sq miles)
Population: 128,000,000
Language: Japanese
Religions: Shinto, Buddhist
Currency: Yen

Temple statue at Nikko, Honshu.

Map labels:

SEA OF JAPAN (EAST SEA)

Tokyo skyscrapers
Electronics
Tuna
TOKYO
BRONZE BUDDHA (KAMAKURA)
Macaque
Kawasaki
Yokohama
Electronics
Skiing
Mt Fuji 3,776 m
Shizuoka
Tea terraces
Cherry blossom
Nagano
Serow
Toyama
Sumo wrestler
Fukui
Nagoya
NAGOYA CASTLE
Cars
Bullet train
Kyoto
Osaka
GOLD PAVILION
Iron and steel
Kobe
Shipbuilding
Citrus fruits
Sardines
Pearls
Oil tanker
Terraced rice fields
Fishing boats
Tottori
OKI ISLANDS
Squid
Shinto dignitary
Okayama
Shinto shrine
Torii gate
Hiroshima
SHIKOKU
Satsumas
Kochi
Crab
Squid
Mackerel
Kabuki theatre
MATSUYAMA CASTLE
Tofu (bean curd)
Miyazaki
Loggerhead turtle
Shrimps
Kitakyushu
Iron and steel
Chemicals
KYUSHU
Kumamoto
Rice planting
Sweet potatoes
Kagoshima
Fukuoka
Anchovies
IKI
TSUSHIMA ISLANDS
Nagasaki
Pottery
GOTO ISLANDS
Shellfish
Octopus
OSUMI ISLANDS
EAST CHINA SEA

OKINAWAN ISLANDS (JAPAN)
Pine-apple
Sugar Cane
Naha
Tourism

IZU ISLANDS

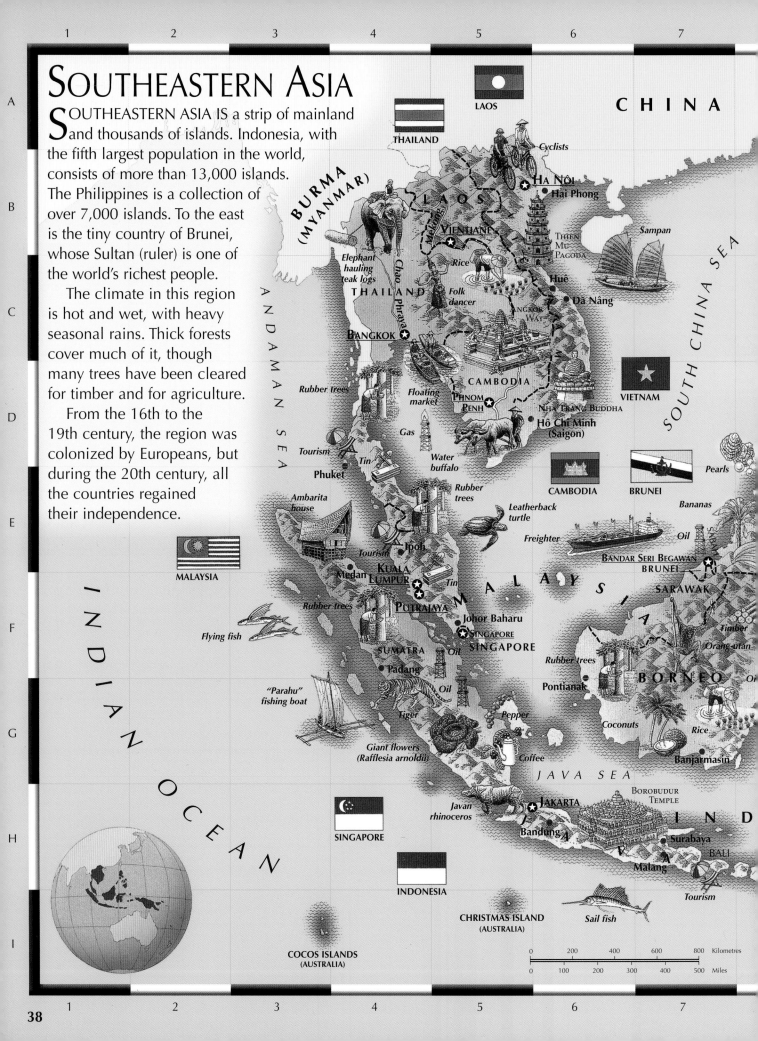

SOUTHEASTERN ASIA

SOUTHEASTERN ASIA IS a strip of mainland and thousands of islands. Indonesia, with the fifth largest population in the world, consists of more than 13,000 islands. The Philippines is a collection of over 7,000 islands. To the east is the tiny country of Brunei, whose Sultan (ruler) is one of the world's richest people.

The climate in this region is hot and wet, with heavy seasonal rains. Thick forests cover much of it, though many trees have been cleared for timber and for agriculture.

From the 16th to the 19th century, the region was colonized by Europeans, but during the 20th century, all the countries regained their independence.

FACTS AND FIGURES

Largest cities:
Manila (Philippines), 10,993,374;
Jakarta (Indonesia), 8,576,788;
Bangkok (Thailand), 5,768,014;
Ho Chi-Minh (Vietnam,
previously called Saigon),
4,331,288.
Highest mountain:
Puncak Jaya (Indonesia),
5,040 m (16,503 ft).
Largest island:
New Guinea, 808,510 sq km
(312,168 sq miles).
Longest river:
Mekong, 4,184 km
(2,600 miles).

BRUNEI
Capital: Bandar Seri Begawan
Area: 5,765 sq km (2,225 sq miles)
Population: 374,000
Languages: Malay, English
Religions: Muslim, Buddhist

CAMBODIA
Capital: Phnom Pénh
Area: 181,035 sq km (69,881 sq miles)
Population: 14,100,000
Languages: Khmer
Religion: Buddhist

EAST TIMOR
Capital: Dili
Area: 14,874 sq km (5,756 sq miles)
Population: 947,000
Languages: Tetum, Indonesian, Portuguese
Religions: Christian

INDONESIA
Capital: Jakarta
Area: 1,904,569 sq km (735,412 sq miles)
Population: 223,000,000
Language: Indonesian
Religion: Muslim

LAOS
Capital: Vientiane
Area: 236,800 sq km (91,435 sq miles)

Population: 5,900,000
Language: Lao
Religion: Buddhist

MALAYSIA
Capital: Kuala Lumpur/Putrajaya
Area: 329,749 sq km (127,326 sq miles)
Population: 25,300,000
Languages: Malay, English, Chinese
Religions: Muslim, Buddhist

PAPUA NEW GUINEA
Capital: Port Moresby
Area: 462,840 sq km (178,716 sq miles)
Population: 5,900,000
Languages: English, numerous others
Religion: Christian

PHILIPPINES
Capital: Manila
Area: 300,000 sq km (115,839 sq miles)
Population: 83,100,000

Languages: Filipino, English, Spanish
Religion: Christian

SINGAPORE
Capital: Singapore
Area: 618 sq km (239 sq miles)
Population: 4,300,000
Languages: Malay, Chinese, English
Religion: Taoist, Buddhist

THAILAND
Capital: Bangkok
Area: 513,115 sq km (198,129 sq miles)
Population: 64,200,000
Language: Thai
Religion: Buddhist

VIETNAM
Capital: Ha Nôi
Area: 329,558 sq km (127,252 sq miles)
Population: 84,200,000
Languages: Vietnamese, Chinese
Religion: Buddhist

MAP QUIZ

- Perahu fishing boats sail along the coast of which country?
- Offshore oil is responsible for the fabulous wealth of which tiny Southeast Asian nation?
- The Mekong River runs through two countries on the map. Can you name them?
- What sea lies off Vietnam?
- Where is the Buddhist temple of Angkor Wat?

TAIWAN

MANILA
LUZON
Rice terraces
Sugar cane
PHILIPPINES
Cebu
PHILIPPINES
Monkey-eating eagle
Coral reefs
MINDANAO
Davao
Zamboanga
Vinta boat
Coral reefs

PACIFIC OCEAN

CELEBES SEA
Coconuts
Sago palms
MOLUCCAS
Oil
Oil
Toraja house
Shrimps
Nutmeg
CERAM SEA
CERAM
CELEBES
Cloves
Coffee
Crabs
Tree kangaroo
Makassar
BANDA SEA
INDONESIA
Komodo dragon
Maize
FLORES
DILI
PART OF EAST TIMOR
EAST TIMOR
SUMBA
Kupang
EAST TIMOR

Sago palms
Tuna
Jayapura
NEW GUINEA
Spirit house
Coconuts
PUNCAK JAYA 5,040 M
New Guinea native
PAPUA NEW GUINEA
Mt Wilhelm 4,509 M
NEW BRITAIN
Asmat warriors
Bird of paradise
Dancer and drum
PORT MORESBY
PAPUA NEW GUINEA

ARAFURA SEA
TIMOR SEA
AUSTRALIA

CHINA AND NORTHEASTERN ASIA

MORE PEOPLE LIVE in China than in any other country. China has over one billion inhabitants, so one person in every five in the world is Chinese. China is also the world's third largest country, after the Russian Federation and Canada. Most people live in the east of China, where the climate is wet and the land is fertile. In most places the farms are owned by each village, so everyone works on them and shares the harvest.

Tibet lies in the highlands of southwest China at an average height of 4,500 m (14,800 ft) above sea level. This is higher than most mountains in Europe and the United States. The Himalayas, the world's highest mountains, stretch along the border between China and India.

After a long civil war in China, a communist government was formed in 1949 by Mao Zedong. The defeated nationalists set up a rival Republic of China on the island of Taiwan, which is still independent. The province of Hong Kong, once a British colony, became part of China in 1997. In Korea, a war was fought in the 1950s between communist and non-communist forces. Korea is now divided into two countries, North Korea and South Korea.

RUSSIAN

MONGOLIA

LAKE UVS

KAZAKHSTAN

Sheep and goats

Oil

Oil

Oil

Iron and steel

M O N

Yaks

LAKE CHARUS

Gazelle

Goats

KYRGYZSTAN

Gas

Kashgar (Kashi)

Kuqa

TIEN SHAN

Ürümqi

Wheat

Cotton

Cotton

Cotton

TAKLIMAKAN DESERT

LOP NUR (SALT BED)

Oil

Oil

Oil

Space rocket launch site

Shache

Yecheng

C H I

Yumen

Han dynasty bronze horse

KUNLUN SHAN

TSAIDAM BASIN

K2 (MT GODWIN AUSTEN) 8,611 M

Vultures

TIBETAN PLATEAU

TIBET

Snow leopard

Takin (wild ox)

Himalayan tahr (wild goat)

Making yak butter

Yaks

Yaks

INDIA

HIMALAYAS

POTALA PALACE

Prayer flags

Pano

NEPAL

Lhasa

Brahmaputra

Tibetan monk

Yangtze

MT EVEREST 8,850 M

BHUTAN

INDIA

Red panda

Salween

CHINA

Mekong

MAP QUIZ

- Where is the source of the the region's longest river, the Yangtze, which flows into the East China Sea?

- In which country would you find the Gobi Desert?

- Name the three bodies of water that surround North and South Korea.

- What kind of animal is a tahr?

- Of which small island country is T'aipei the capital?

- Yaks are traditional beasts of burden in Tibet. What else are they used for?

- What is the alternative name for the mountain known as K2?

Toba

BURMA (MYANMAR)

Te

THAILAND

40

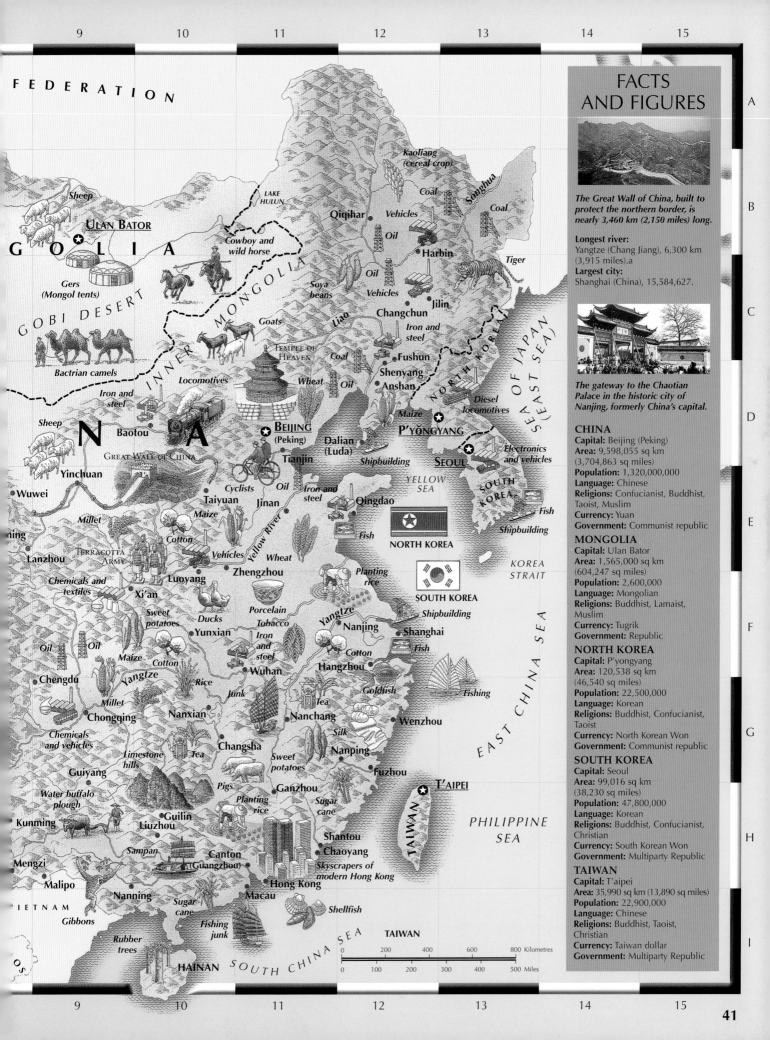

FEDERATION

A

GOLIA

ULAN BATOR

Sheep

Gers
(Mongol tents)

GOBI DESERT

Bactrian camels

LAKE HULUN

Cowboy and
wild horse

INNER MONGOLIA

Goats

Soya beans

Qiqihar

Vehicles

Oil

Kaoliang
(cereal crop)

Coal

Songhua

Coal

Harbin

Tiger

Oil

Vehicles

Changchun

Jilin

Iron and steel

Liao

SEA OF JAPAN (EAST SEA)

NORTH KOREA

Iron and
steel

Locomotives

Temple of Heaven

Goats

Wheat

Coal

Oil

Fushun

Shenyang

Anshan

Diesel
locomotives

N

Baotou

GREAT WALL OF CHINA

Sheep

Yinchuan

Wuwei

A

BEIJING
(Peking)

Dalian
(Luda)

Tianjin

Cyclists

Oil

Maize

P'YŎNGYANG

SEOUL

Shipbuilding

Maize

Electronics
and vehicles

SOUTH KOREA

YELLOW SEA

Millet

Lanzhou

TERRACOTTA ARMY

Cotton

Taiyuan

Jinan

Iron and
steel

Qingdao

Fish

Fish

NORTH KOREA

Shipbuilding

KOREA STRAIT

Vehicles

Yellow River

Wheat

Maize

Chemicals and
textiles

Xi'an

Sweet
potatoes

Luoyang

Zhengzhou

Ducks

Porcelain

Tobacco

Iron and
steel

Planting
rice

SOUTH KOREA

Shipbuilding

Oil

Oil

Maize

Cotton

Yangtze

Chengdu

Millet

Yunxian

Yangtze

Nanjing

Shanghai

Fish

Cotton

Wuhan

Hangzhou

Rice

Goldfish

Fishing

Junk

Chongqing

Nanxian

Tea

Nanchang

Silk

Wenzhou

Chemicals
and vehicles

Guiyang

Limestone
hills

Changsha

Tea

Sweet
potatoes

Nanping

Water buffalo
plough

Kunming

Guilin

Liuzhou

Pigs

Planting
rice

Ganzhou

Fuzhou

T'AIPEI

EAST CHINA SEA

PHILIPPINE SEA

Sampan

Sugar
cane

TAIWAN

Mengzi

Malipo

Nanning

Sugar
cane

Canton
(Guangzhou)

Macau

Shantou

Chaoyang

Skyscrapers of
modern Hong Kong

Hong Kong

Shellfish

VIETNAM

Gibbons

Rubber
trees

HAINAN

Fishing
junk

SOUTH CHINA SEA

TAIWAN

0   200   400   600   800 Kilometres

0   100   200   300   400   500 Miles

FACTS AND FIGURES

The Great Wall of China, built to protect the northern border, is nearly 3,460 km (2,150 miles) long.

Longest river:
Yangtze (Chang Jiang), 6,300 km (3,915 miles).a
Largest city:
Shanghai (China), 15,584,627.

The gateway to the Chaotian Palace in the historic city of Nanjing, formerly China's capital.

CHINA
Capital: Beijing (Peking)
Area: 9,598,055 sq km (3,704,863 sq miles)
Population: 1,320,000,000
Language: Chinese
Religions: Confucianist, Buddhist, Taoist, Muslim
Currency: Yuan
Government: Communist republic

MONGOLIA
Capital: Ulan Bator
Area: 1,565,000 sq km (604,247 sq miles)
Population: 2,600,000
Language: Mongolian
Religions: Buddhist, Lamaist, Muslim
Currency: Tugrik
Government: Republic

NORTH KOREA
Capital: P'yongyang
Area: 120,538 sq km (46,540 sq miles)
Population: 22,500,000
Language: Korean
Religions: Buddhist, Confucianist, Taoist
Currency: North Korean Won
Government: Communist republic

SOUTH KOREA
Capital: Seoul
Area: 99,016 sq km (38,230 sq miles)
Population: 47,800,000
Language: Korean
Religions: Buddhist, Confucianist, Christian
Currency: South Korean Won
Government: Multiparty Republic

TAIWAN
Capital: T'aipei
Area: 35,990 sq km (13,890 sq miles)
Population: 22,900,000
Language: Chinese
Religions: Buddhist, Taoist, Christian
Currency: Taiwan dollar
Government: Multiparty Republic

AFRICA

A FLAT PLATEAU broken by mountain ranges, Africa stretches about 4,000 km (2,500 miles) north and south of the equator. Dominating north Africa are the Mediterranean coastline and the Sahara Desert; to the south are the grasslands of east Africa, the rainforest of the Congo river basin and the farmlands of Kenya, Uganda and Tanzania.

Some African countries have agricultural economies: maize, coffee, tea, fruit, tobacco and cotton are typical crops. Others are rich in gold, diamonds, oil, copper and iron. Many regions, though, are desperately poor, and their people suffer constantly from disease and famine.

MAP QUIZ

- The highest peak in Africa is Mt Kilimanjaro. Where is it?
- In what country can you see the pyramids at Giza, which were built as tombs for ancient rulers?
- Can you name the world's longest river, which flows through Africa into the Mediterranean Sea?
- The largest desert on earth is also on this continent. What is it called?
- What is a felucca?
- Which country has three capital cities?

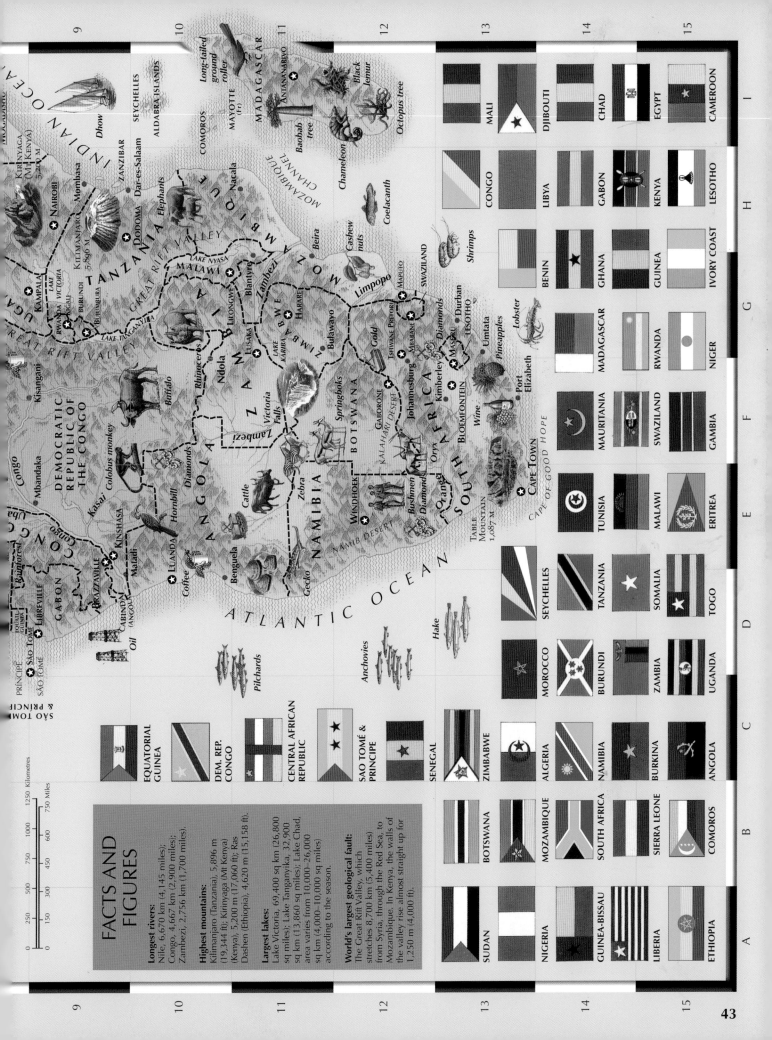

FACTS AND FIGURES

Longest rivers:
Nile, 6,670 km (4,145 miles); Congo, 4,667 km (2,900 miles); Zambezi, 2,756 km (1,700 miles).

Highest mountains:
Kilimanjaro (Tanzania), 5,896 m (19,344 ft); Kirinyaga (Mt Kenya) (Kenya), 5,200 m (17,060 ft); Ras Dashen (Ethiopia), 4,620 m (15,158 ft).

Largest lakes:
Lake Victoria, 69,400 sq km (26,800 sq miles); Lake Tanganyika, 32,900 sq km (13,860 sq miles); Lake Chad, area varies from 10,000–26,000 sq km (4,000–10,000 sq miles) according to the season.

World's largest geological fault:
The Great Rift Valley, which stretches 8,700 km (5,400 miles) from Syria, through the Red Sea, to Mozambique. In Kenya, the walls of the valley rise almost straight up for 1,250 m (4,000 ft).

AUSTRALIA

AUSTRALIA IS A country and a continent. Much of it is hot and dry, especially in the sparsely populated central deserts. Most people live where the climate is wetter, east of the Great Dividing Range and on the island of Tasmania. Two-thirds of all Australians live in cities, particularly Sydney, Melbourne, and Brisbane. The population of Australia is only 21 million people, compared with 278 million in the United States.

Millions of years ago, Australia drifted away from the other continents, so many plants and animals that evolved there are not found anywhere else. Some mammals, such as kangaroos, are marsupials: they rear their young in pouches on their stomachs.

The first inhabitants appeared about 100,000 years ago and Aboriginal Australians are their descendants. Europeans did not arrive until around 200 years ago. Since 1945 the population has doubled, with people coming to Australia from many parts of the world.

MAP QUIZ

- Uluru (Ayers Rock) is near which group of mountains?

- Name the two coastal cities joined by the Indian-Pacific Railway.

- Where would you find an international opera house whose design was inspired by sailing ships?

- The Port Arthur Penal Settlement is located on which island?

- What is the common name for an Australian wild dog?

- Which remote town provides a base for the flying doctor service?

- Can you find the place where a meteorite landed in Australia?

AURA SEA

CORAL SEA

GULF OF CARPENTARIA

TORRES STRAIT

Aboriginal dancers

GROOTE EYLANDT

Aboriginal cave paintings

Coral reef

Water buffalo

HERN ITORY

BARKLY TABLELAND

Cattle

Green turtle

Sugar cane

Coral reef

The Devil's Marbles

Cairns

Scuba diving

Cattle

Mount Isa

Road train

Townsville

RALIA

MACDONNELL RANGES

Coal

Mackay

Coral reef

Alice Springs

Flying doctor

Sheep

QUEENSLAND

Sugar cane

RANGES

Wallabies

Sheep

Rockhampton

H AUSTRALIA

Opals

LAKE EYRE

Grains

Coal

LAKE TORRENS

Sheep

River red gum tree

Darling

Koalas

Lyrebird

Brisbane skyscrapers

Woomera

Sapphires

Brisbane

LAKE GAIRDNER

Broken Hill

NEW SOUTH

Pineapples

Surfers Paradise

Port Augusta

Kookaburra

Tamworth

Bananas

Whyalla

WALES

Windsurfing

Iron and steel

Platypus

Coal

Iron and steel

Paddle steamer

Newcastle

Cars

Mildura

Murrumbidgee

Wollongong

GHT

Adelaide

Murray

Wagga Wagga

Sydney

Shipbuilding

Pelicans

CANBERRA

SYDNEY OPERA HOUSE AND BRIDGE

Albury

Great white shark

Wine

VICTORIA

Skiing

Surfing

AUSTRALIAN CAPITAL TERRITORY

Rock lobster

Timber

Bendigo

Ballarat

Melbourne

Geelong

OCEAN

Fairy penguins

Horse racing

Sharks

BASS STRAIT

Sailing

TASMAN SEA

Tasmanian devil

TASMANIA

Port Arthur Penal Settlement

Apples

Hobart

AUSTRALIA

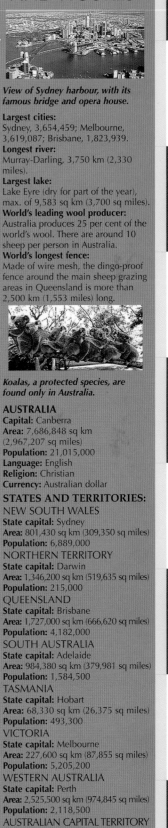

FACTS AND FIGURES

View of Sydney harbour, with its famous bridge and opera house.

Largest cities:
Sydney, 3,654,459; Melbourne, 3,619,087; Brisbane, 1,823,939.
Longest river:
Murray-Darling, 3,750 km (2,330 miles).
Largest lake:
Lake Eyre (dry for part of the year), max. of 9,583 sq km (3,700 sq miles).
World's leading wool producer:
Australia produces 25 per cent of the world's wool. There are around 10 sheep per person in Australia.
World's longest fence:
Made of wire mesh, the dingo-proof fence around the main sheep grazing areas in Queensland is more than 2,500 km (1,553 miles) long.

Koalas, a protected species, are found only in Australia.

AUSTRALIA
Capital: Canberra
Area: 7,686,848 sq km (2,967,207 sq miles)
Population: 21,015,000
Language: English
Religion: Christian
Currency: Australian dollar

STATES AND TERRITORIES:
NEW SOUTH WALES
State capital: Sydney
Area: 801,430 sq km (309,350 sq miles)
Population: 6,889,000
NORTHERN TERRITORY
State capital: Darwin
Area: 1,346,200 sq km (519,635 sq miles)
Population: 215,000
QUEENSLAND
State capital: Brisbane
Area: 1,727,000 sq km (666,620 sq miles)
Population: 4,182,000
SOUTH AUSTRALIA
State capital: Adelaide
Area: 984,380 sq km (379,981 sq miles)
Population: 1,584,500
TASMANIA
State capital: Hobart
Area: 68,330 sq km (26,375 sq miles)
Population: 493,300
VICTORIA
State capital: Melbourne
Area: 227,600 sq km (87,855 sq miles)
Population: 5,205,200
WESTERN AUSTRALIA
State capital: Perth
Area: 2,525,500 sq km (974,845 sq miles)
Population: 2,118,500
AUSTRALIAN CAPITAL TERRITORY
State capital: Canberra
Area: 2,432 sq km (939 sq miles)
Population: 339,900

New Zealand

MADE UP OF two main islands – North Island and South Island – New Zealand lies about 1,600 km (1,000 miles) off Australia. Most people live on North Island, which has a tropical climate.

The first settlers were the Maoris, who arrived from Polynesia around AD 900. The first European was the Dutch explorer Abel Tasman in 1642. New Zealand became a British colony in 1840 and gained independence in 1907. Today, the population is mainly a mix of Maoris and people of British descent.

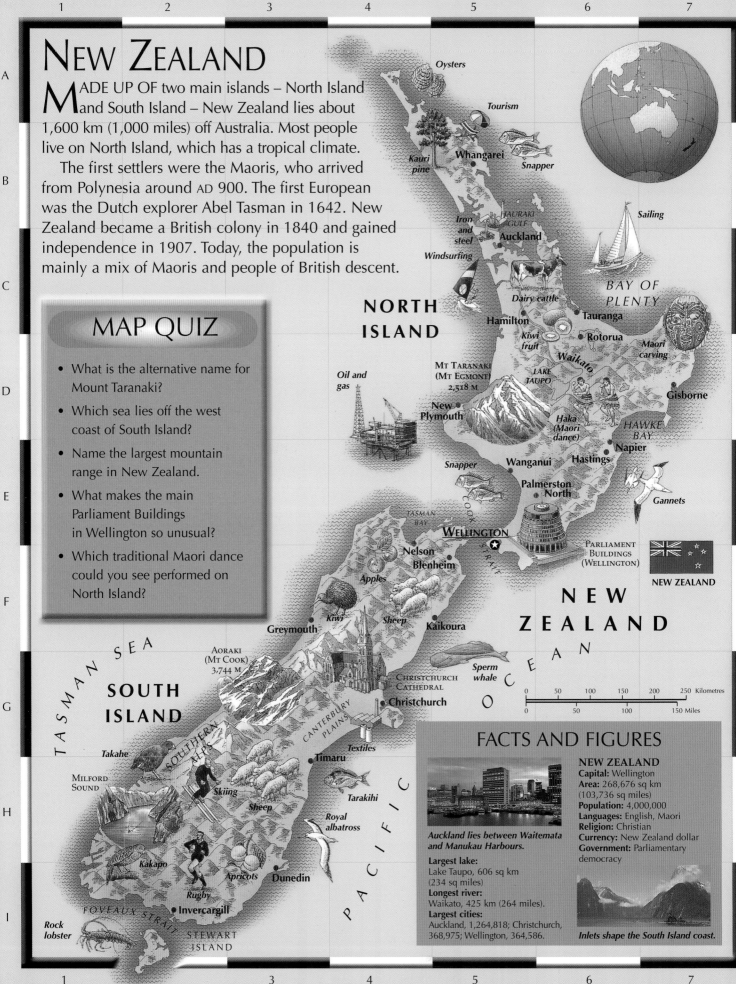

MAP QUIZ

- What is the alternative name for Mount Taranaki?

- Which sea lies off the west coast of South Island?

- Name the largest mountain range in New Zealand.

- What makes the main Parliament Buildings in Wellington so unusual?

- Which traditional Maori dance could you see performed on North Island?

Map labels

Oysters
Tourism
Kauri pine
Whangarei
Snapper
Sailing
HAURAKI GULF
Iron and steel
Auckland
Windsurfing
NORTH ISLAND
BAY OF PLENTY
Dairy cattle
Tauranga
Hamilton
Kiwi fruit
Rotorua
Maori carving
Waikato
Oil and gas
MT TARANAKI (MT EGMONT) 2,518 M
LAKE TAUPO
New Plymouth
Haka (Maori dance)
Gisborne
HAWKE BAY
Napier
Snapper
Wanganui
Hastings
Palmerston North
Gannets
TASMAN BAY
WELLINGTON
COOK STRAIT
Nelson
Blenheim
PARLIAMENT BUILDINGS (WELLINGTON)
NEW ZEALAND
Apples
NEW ZEALAND OCEAN
Kiwi
Sheep
Kaikoura
Greymouth
AORAKI (MT COOK) 3,744 M
CHRISTCHURCH CATHEDRAL
Sperm whale
SOUTH ISLAND
Christchurch
TASMAN SEA
Takahe
CANTERBURY PLAINS
SOUTHERN ALPS
Textiles
MILFORD SOUND
Skiing
Timaru
Tarakihi
Sheep
Royal albatross
PACIFIC
Kakapo
Apricots
Dunedin
Rugby
Invercargill
FOVEAUX STRAIT
Rock lobster
STEWART ISLAND

FACTS AND FIGURES

Auckland lies between Waitemata and Manukau Harbours.

NEW ZEALAND
Capital: Wellington
Area: 268,676 sq km (103,736 sq miles)
Population: 4,000,000
Languages: English, Maori
Religion: Christian
Currency: New Zealand dollar
Government: Parliamentary democracy

Largest lake:
Lake Taupo, 606 sq km (234 sq miles)
Longest river:
Waikato, 425 km (264 miles).
Largest cities:
Auckland, 1,264,818; Christchurch, 368,975; Wellington, 364,586.

Inlets shape the South Island coast.

Scale: 0 50 100 150 200 250 Kilometres
0 50 100 150 Miles

INDEX

This index contains the most important place and feature names. The page number is given in **bold** type after the place name. The grid reference follows in lighter type.

48